Endorsements:

"What if everything you've ever dreamed of in your relationship with God is already yours to enjoy? What if you just don't realize how good you've got it? That's the radical message in The Gospel Uncut by Jeremy White, a pastor who is not afraid to proclaim the gospel of grace, plainly and without compromise. Read this book to see you are clean and close to your God. Read this book to relax and enjoy your Jesus. He loves you so!"

Andrew Farley
bestselling author of "The Naked Gospel" and host of "Andrew Farley LIVE" on Sirius XM

"Everyone looks for that just-right book, the one that will quickly illuminate and invigorate, and which will resolve odd questions that have plagued for years. This is that book. I'm not kidding. The Gospel Uncut is truly a treasure that is both breathtaking and timely! Jeremy White skillfully leads the reader out of tangled wonderings about God and into the clear and easy rest and love that Jesus offers to all. If you're looking for treasure, get this book!"

Ralph Harris
author of "God's Astounding Opinion of You" and President of LifeCourse Ministries.

The Gospel Uncut

Learning to Rest in the Grace of God

Jeremy White

WESTBOW
P R E S S
A DIVISION OF THOMAS NELSON

WestBow Press books may be ordered through booksellers or by contacting:

WestBow Press
A Division of Thomas Nelson
1663 Liberty Drive
Bloomington, IN 47403
www.westbowpress.com
1-(866) 928-1240

Unless otherwise noted, all Scripture is taken from the NIV (1984 ed.)

ISBN: 978-1-4497-6566-8 (e)
ISBN: 978-1-4497-6567-5 (sc)
ISBN: 978-1-4497-6568-2 (hc)

Library of Congress Control Number: 2012916081

Printed in the United States of America

WestBow Press rev. date: 11/6/2012

For April,
Who has taught me more about living the grace
life than any theologian ever could.
I love you beyond words.
Thanks for being Jesus to me.

Contents

Introduction:
Grace – More Amazing than You Thought!

I think I might know why you picked up this book. It's not because I'm famous or amazing. In fact, I'm a pastor of a local church in Northern California, a single voice among a chorus out there writing, speaking, blogging and pontificating about any one of a thousand different things. So why on earth would you drop even one moment of your precious time on a book written by a guy you've probably never met and have no automatic reason to trust?

Here's my guess: you and I are a lot alike.

Having snooped around the church world for awhile we probably share some similar questions, discomforts and experiences. Then again, maybe you are investigating Jesus or are new to the Christian faith and you sense the goings on of a bait-and-switch scheme – a too-good-to-be-true offer of God's grace and forgiveness on the front end of the deal that you fear will inevitably come with all kinds of religious fine print attached to the flip side. Perhaps you are drawn to Jesus the Person, but you've seen the dark side of religion and don't want anything to do with it. I've known that eerie feeling all too well.

My parents became "Jesus Freaks" in the mid 1970's during the Jesus Movement. I was two years old when my dad and mom decided they were going to try to raise me with an awareness of Jesus Christ. They gave it their best shot and for that I am grateful. My spiritual foundations were largely influenced by my exposure to so many people of faith throughout my early life.

Nevertheless, growing up in the church can be a very disillusioning experience. Perhaps you can relate to feeling as though God were something like a cosmic bill-collector constantly harassing you to make good on late payments and unfulfilled commitments. Maybe you grew up envisioning God along the lines of an irritable parochial school teacher hovering over your shoulder just waiting to smack your knuckles with a yardstick for the slightest act of indiscretion.

I'm guessing you have always wanted to believe that God *really is* the unconditional Lover you have heard preachers talk about, but you have been unable to become convinced of it at the gut-level. And quite possibly you find yourself today wondering how much of what you believe about God's character is true and real, and how much is just a mess of debris you picked up along the way.

Prior to becoming a lead pastor I had served as a youth pastor for 14 years. Throughout my ministry to teenagers and young adults I sought to proclaim and demonstrate a message of God's grace to many students who were burdened by doubt, guilt, pain, rejection and legalism. As imperfect as my efforts were, one thing was certain: I typically preached a far better message of God's grace toward others than I ever embraced for myself.

This may sound a little weird to you, because it raises an obvious question: "Was I being disingenuous when I spent all those years reassuring others of God's love?" I have asked myself that very question, and the answer is categorically "no".

For years, I truly believed that the Biblical message of the gospel was one of *irrationally* free, *infinitely* available and *irreversibly* stubborn love, forgiveness and grace for anyone who would receive it by simple faith. Yet for reasons that until recently I did not understand, I could never fully accept those realities for myself at the heart-level.

Relentless perfectionism and self-criticism, haunting doubt and ongoing struggles with sin kept me ever questioning my validity as a

Christian, much less as a vocational member of the clergy! Thankfully, I remained faithful to the public proclamation of grace, but my private inability to accept its reality on a deeply experiential level was quite another story!

As if these mounting inner conflicts were not enough, pressure was added by the fact that often my particular array of gifts and talents would tend to draw outward kudos from others. This may sound like a positive thing, but the fact is that when large numbers of people know you almost exclusively from the hour per week they see you on a stage using your God-given abilities, it is easy to find yourself drowning in a sea of surface-level relationships. That's how I felt during many seasons along the way.

Don't get me wrong. This was not the fault of the wonderful people around me. In most cases their affirmations were sincere attempts to give God credit for the way He would use me to help them understand the Bible or grow spiritually. They weren't being the least bit sinister by thanking or encouraging me.

The problem was with me, and with the personality-driven culture in which members of the clergy can often erroneously be viewed as "superstar Christians". When people begin to affirm and follow your leadership, it is easy to fall into the quandary of being the most popular guy in the room while simultaneously feeling like the loneliest.

The more I served and used my gifts, the more affirmation I received. The more affirmation I received, the more validity I felt in my life and calling. The more validity I felt in my life and calling, the more it freaked me out to be honest with anyone about my doubts, fears, sins and struggles.

While I am sharing a part of my spiritual journey here in the opening of this book, I want you to know that the pages that follow are not primarily about me. In the pages that follow I *will* share about some personal experiences along the journey. I *will* strive to be transparent about my struggles in hopes that you can learn from my errors or take comfort that you are not alone in yours. And while my intense desire is that this will be one of the most encouraging books you will ever read, ultimately the book is not about you either.

This book is about God and His good news – the gospel uncut – and about how easy it is for us to distort and diminish the purity, simplicity and beauty of that message by attaching to it the baggage of our own experiences, presuppositions, and legalism. In other words, by adding our own "edits" to the gospel.

Nothing New Here

This editorializing of the gospel is nothing new. Nearly two thousand years ago the Apostle Paul was writing to confront the false teachings of a religious sect which was spreading the message that a person must be *circumcised* in accordance with the custom of Abraham in order to rest assured of their salvation and be a truly "good Christian." These folks lived in a region called Galatia.

Paul passionately reassured the Galatians that there was absolutely no need to add circumcision – or any other human endeavor – to their simple trust in the resurrected Christ. Assurance of salvation and the abundant life that goes with it come only through faith in the finished work of Jesus. This was and is the uncut gospel that Paul and the Apostles preached and defended against other forms of legalism.

Our generation is likewise responsible to expose and correct the modern "edits" of this gospel that leave scraps of its beautiful simplicity on the cutting room floor in our day. That is the ultimate aim of the pages that follow.

Although we will cover a lot of ground, this book is not an attempt to answer every question or address every nuance related to the gospel. Others have tried that approach and failed, and I want to attempt to avoid their ranks by admitting at the outset that I cannot in one volume (nor in one lifetime) exhaust the awesome splendor of amazing grace.

What I *do* hope to accomplish is this: that those who have been worried and wearied by the parched desert of religious legalism in any form, whether self-inflicted or otherwise, will receive from this book something that feels like a cup of cold water offered in Jesus' name. And with it a refreshed invitation to cast off the shackles of burdensome religiosity in favor of an uncut gospel that was never intended to confuse, mislead or be watered-down with the joy-robbing huffing and puffing so many of us have attached to it.

How to Navigate these Pages

The Gospel Uncut is divided into three distinct segments. Part one is called *(Un)Load* because in this section we will toss onto the table a number of issues we need to discuss about various modern "edits" of the original gospel of Jesus Christ. Sometimes the best way to chart our course is to first consider where we have been and where we are at right now.

Section two is called *(Un)Learn*. Here we will uncover and reinforce the precious reality of God's amazing grace toward His children, "un-learning" some lies and half-truths by rethinking them in light of the actual teachings of Jesus and the Apostles.

The third and final section is titled *(Un)Leash*. In this segment we will discover the practical power of grace in the real world, on both a personal and communal level, as well as demonstrate how God's grace works in our lives to ensure that we actually experience the abundant life Jesus promised.

Whether you are investigating the claims of Jesus for the first time, are new to the faith, or are battle-scarred from a life lived in the trenches of doubt and disillusionment, this book is for you. May a new generation of passionate contenders return to the breathtaking freedom of God's grace, essentially picking up where the great Protestant Reformers left off! What do I mean by this? You'll find out in chapter one. But first a few words of clarification...

A Word Before

If you have followed much of the recent discussion about the nature of the gospel and its myriad of implications for socially redemptive action (i.e. care for the poor, justice for the oppressed, etc.), I sense a need to define what I mean when I use terms like "justification", "salvation" and "gospel" in the context of this book.

First, I affirm with many fellow believers, pastors and leaders that the implications of the gospel carry far greater significance than merely "making sure I go to Heaven when I die." Many of the criticisms related to our reductionist mindset toward God and spirituality are points well taken.

I believe that the uncut gospel is potentially as powerful for the redemption of cultures and communities as it is for the spiritual re-birth of individuals. We are amiss if we assume that the only focus of Christianity is about us personally getting to heaven someday.

The needless rift between the realities of social redemption and spiritual re-birth has served to widen the chasm between so-called "conservative" and "liberal" followers of Jesus. I am thankful that many theologically conservative leaders among my generation are taking up the mantle to bring the best of both intentions together with unwavering fidelity to Biblical revelation.

Perhaps God will allow me to express my thoughts on these

matters in a future volume. In the meantime I want the reader of this book to know that I am

a) Aware of Christ's socially redemptive intentions for the gospel, and
b) I embrace them and seek to pastor a church that is compassionately engaged in them.

That being said, I also believe that the recent epiphanies among Evangelicals related to social justice and kingdom living do not in any way negate the myriad of Scriptural teachings related to the necessity of spiritual re-birth, individual salvation and a personal relationship with God available exclusively by grace through faith in Christ.

Those of us who still believe in places called Heaven and Hell are often accused of being "so heavenly minded that we're no earthly good," as though we are merely sitting around waiting for the Rapture while we let the culture go to hell in a hand-basket. There may be a few professing Christians who are that myopic, but for the most part, this caricature is unfounded and unfair.

> God wants to forgive sinners eternally, replace our inherent wickedness with Christ's righteousness and offer us new and eternal life to be experienced beginning in the here and now!

The Scriptures teach that God *does* want human beings to spend eternity with Him in His heavenly kingdom. According to the Bible, there *is* such a thing as being saved from an eternal judgment called Hell and going to Heaven instead. In fact, I believe that the focus of the New Testament offer of salvation continues to be plain and simple: God wants to forgive sinners eternally, replace our inherent wickedness with Christ's righteousness and offer us new and eternal life to be experienced beginning in the here and now!

For the purposes of this book, unless I specifically state otherwise, whenever I use familiar salvation terminology I am referring to the reality that a holy God redeems sinners on the basis of His grace alone through faith alone in Christ alone, immersing them forever into relationship with Himself and thereby granting total forgiveness, new life and the promise of a heavenly future.

It is the believing and receiving of this saving gift of grace that separates real Christianity from any other belief system in the world. It was this grace that Luther and the Reformers so passionately attempted to articulate and defend. Thus, it is this grace alone that not only assures us of our eternal future, but of our joy and security in the day-to-day challenges of this life.

If you are like the many believers I have known who often feel beat up, broken down or ripped off by a bait-and-switch version of Christianity that promised a free gift only to tack on the external pressures of performance when you weren't looking, may this book reorient you toward the uncut, life-giving message of the cross and resurrection. Namely, that nothing can "separate us from the love of God which is in Christ Jesus our Lord."

Acknowledgements

Writing books is a much more serious undertaking than one might expect. I am deeply indebted to the following people who contributed – knowingly or unknowingly – to the contents of this book.

To my family, who allowed me to invest many hours of my "spare time" writing, re-writing, researching, reading, editing and finalizing the manuscript for this book. April, Justin, Jesse and Jake…my life as a dad and husband is better than I ever dreamed and it is all because of you!

To the incredible staff and membership of Valley Church, serving as one of your pastors is a joy indescribable. Thank you for walking with me down the path of His glorious grace. I pray that we will take many more steps down that path together!

To grace-focused authors and leaders like Andrew Farley, Ralph Harris, Charles Bing, Charles Swindoll, Doug Fields, Philip Yancey, Brennan Manning, Joseph Dillow, Charles Ryrie, Zane Hodges, Bob George, Neil Anderson, John Lynch, Wayne Jacobsen, David Seamonds, Mike Yaconelli (now in heaven), David Gregory, John Eldridge, John Best, Mick Mooney, Dan Stone, Charles Stanley, Larry Crabb, Jud Wilhite, Sandra Wilson, Bill and Anabel Gillham, James Fowler, Frank Friedmann and many others who have greatly contributed along the way in helping me to discover and live the grace life more fully! We may see a few issues from different angles – but we are united in our quest to proclaim the Gospel Uncut!

To professors like Dr. Keith Stone, Dr. George Gunn, Dr. Steven Brown, Dr. David Nicholas and Rev. Al Franklin for grounding me in the knowledge of grace as a young man striving to get through Bible College.

To the incredible and gifted senior pastors I served under during the many years I was a youth pastor, each of whom taught me different unforgettable things about God's grace – Rev. Bob Langfield, Rev. Ben Pent, Rev. Tim Puentes and Dr. Raleigh Galgan.

To Dan Porter, my own youth pastor who is now in glory with Jesus and who first introduced me to God as grace-giver...I miss you and will see you again one day!

To Dr. Gordon Luff, whose personal investment in my life and ministry to youth has been immeasurable.

To those who read, discussed and helped me refine the ideas and contents of this book through many conversations and much fellowship – Russ Elder, Kevin Anderson, Pastor Darren Paulson, Pastor Michael Lamantia, Pastor Josh Fuller, Pastors David and Cathy Hildebrand, Pastor Brian Logue, and Mom. I love you all (with a special shout-out to Mom).

To the good folks at Westbow Press, A Division of Thomas Nelson – for believing in my vision for the book and helping me with publication... may God use this project to set captives free!

PART ONE: (UN)LOAD -
Exposing Some Modern "Edits" of the Gospel

Chapter 1: Contenders

I ronically, the God who identifies Himself as love has entrusted His people with the most offensive message in the world. That message is not *deny yourself* or *take up your cross* or *die to self* or *sell all you have* or *live your faith radically* or *just do something* or *give until it hurts* or *no pain, no gain*.

The message is *much* more offensive than any of those predictable mantras. The most offensive message in the world is simply *grace*. No matter how gently, lovingly, or patiently one presents it, grace offends the legalist in everyone. The central call of the uncut gospel is really a message to the Pharisee in all of us. That call is simply that *"Jesus has done it ALL! Get over yourself, cease from your huffing and puffing and learn to relax in Him!"*

Yesterday and Today

Two thousand years ago, one of Jesus' well-known followers wrote a controversial letter. It was addressed to a group of churches he had helped get started in a region called Galatia, an area located in modern-day Turkey. The man's name was Paul, and he was extremely frustrated, to say the least.

A group of false teachers had come into the area teaching the new Christians things that were in direct opposition to the uncut gospel Paul had taught them. This sectarian group was claiming that in *addition* to simple faith in Christ, the believers of Galatia needed also to conform to various aspects of the Jewish traditions – most notably the Abrahamic custom of circumcision by which the ancient Jews would outwardly demonstrate their conversion.

History affirms that the Galatians were a sadly gullible group of people. Julius Caesar reportedly said of them, "They are fickle, they are fond of change, and they are not to be trusted."[1]

The original people of Galatia came from Gall, which today is France. As they migrated into the area with their Celtic background they hung together throughout the region. They were known to be a people easily swayed by popular philosophy and were extremely prone to "flip-flopping" from one idea to the next.

In fact, we see the stark reality of their fickle nature in Acts 14, where Paul goes into several communities in Galatia including one called Lystra. In that community, Paul performed a miracle for a guy who was disabled, restoring his ability to walk. In response to this supernatural display of power, the Galatians immediately began to worship Paul and even tried to offer a sacrifice to him as though he were a god!

In essence Paul repied, "What the heck are you doing? Don't worship us! We are not gods! We are only human like you are!"[2] But later in the evening on the very same day, a group of false teachers from a neighboring town came along preaching their highly edited version of the gospel. So persuasive were their teachings that they convinced the Galatians – the very folks who were ready to worship Paul earlier that morning – to pick up rocks in order to stone him as a heretic!

Imagine that! They worshiped Paul in the morning, but later in the day they did a complete one-eighty and tried to kill him! They were easily swayed by fine-sounding arguments which appealed to the idea that the uncut gospel Paul taught was simply too good to be true.

Surely there had to be *more* to it than simply believing that Jesus had died and been raised from the dead! Certainly there should be some sort of outward verification that a person was a *true* convert to Christ! Nobody could possibly get off that easily!

In today's religious landscape, we don't typically find people trying to convince their male friends to be circumcised for spiritual reasons. However, we definitely see other variations and "edits" – attempts to *add to* or *subtract from* the work that Jesus has completed for us through His death, burial and resurrection!

Rather than living by simple faith in the Son of God and the power of His Spirit, many believers are taught that there are additional "principles" to be added to the formula if they are going to live successfully as Christians. As Paul set the record straight with the Galatians who were so prone to believing these lies, so every generation of believers is called to "contend for the faith that was once for all entrusted to the saints."[3]

Understanding Where We've Been

In recent editions of his popular modern classic *The Ragamuffin Gospel*, author Brennan Manning writes that when it comes to his bold message of God's amazing grace some of his critics have accused him of essentially "out-reforming" the Reformers.[4] In my opinion, this accusation is the one of the finest compliments a preacher of the gospel could possibly receive! To understand what I mean by this, consider a bit of history as we begin.

Step back in time with me about five centuries. From the perspective of those Christians living during the days of Martin Luther, John Calvin and other disconcerted church leaders of the Enlightenment era, their sixteenth Century messages of were nothing short of earth-shaking.

Beginning with Luther's bold articulations of what we commonly call "justification by faith" (being placed in right relationship with God through faith alone apart from human merit) and in conjunction with major advancements in literacy and communication, a domino effect of seismic proportions began to ripple through the fabric of both church and culture.

This was a time when the State-sponsored Church leaders were mostly chosen by secular authorities in order to control people's lives through religious guilt and manipulation. Luther's ideas were not only a threat to their very false gospel, but also to the dominant influence of major political powers.

As common folks were finally given the opportunity to read the Scriptures for themselves on a mass scale, a great outcry erupted. This emerged into a movement that would forever change the face of global history. That movement was the Protestant Reformation, sparking a new thread of spiritual revival, denominational diversity, and global evangelism.

Which Lenses are We Looking Through?

Although denominational allegiance has waned in recent decades, many in the contemporary Protestant traditions still love to theologically "attach" themselves to the core teachings one or more of their favorite beloved Reformers. With a commitment rivaling (and sometimes seemingly surpassing) their professed love for Jesus Himself, many believers from across the denominational spectrum strongly align their beliefs and practices with their personal heroes of the Reformation Age.

As New Testament scholar Scot McKnight points out, we need to be careful about this. McKnight argues that believers have a conscious choice to make about the lenses we look through when interpreting the Scriptures. We can either read the Bible *through* tradition, or we can read the Bible *with* tradition.

In essence, those who insist on reading the Bible *through* tradition, McKnight says, will tend to believe that because their favorite Christian leader or theologian has spoken on an issue in centuries past, the conversation is now essentially over. To question that perceived reality equates to virtual heresy.[5]

However, McKnight asserts that those who read the Bible *with* tradition tend to do so with a more discerning eye, deeply appreciating the collective witness of those gone before, but realizing that *every* generation must wrestle with, question and re-state its core beliefs based on the ever-multiplying body of research, writing, and reflection available to the universal Body of Christ. The premise is that each succeeding generation is to build upon or refine the witness of those gone before so that in every generation we are actively contending for the faith "once delivered" by the original Apostles and Prophets.[6]

Subjective Interpretation?

Please do not misunderstand what I am saying. I do *not* believe that Scriptural truth is subject to the interpretation of the audience at hand. I am not advocating that we should cease to be confident in our core beliefs, or that truth is relative. In fact, I argue for quite the opposite in the pages that follow.

I am simply agreeing that we need to be as humble as we are bold in our approach to truth, taking into consideration the fact that there is only one all-knowing God in the universe, and we are not Him. While there are clarities in the Bible that have held Christ's followers together for centuries, there are also Divine mysteries and human limitations to be dealt with in approaching the infinite mind of the God those Scriptures reveal.

For some, the idea of reading the Bible *with* rather than *through* tradition is almost unthinkable. In their minds, to question whether a cherished theologian may have had his views even the least bit tainted by cultural surroundings or personal bias can be perceived as the near equivalent to *blasphemy*.

For example, to push back at John Calvin on various points of theology can sometimes lead to the accusation by his modern followers of accepting Pelagianism (an ancient works-based approach to salvation). While these characterizations are demonstrably false and unwarranted, they are nonetheless prevalent among some of the more combative supporters of certain Protestant traditions and theological systems.

Allow me to clarify that I believe the Protestant Reformation was the most significant and positive advancement in our understanding of the gospel that has occurred since the writings of the Apostles themselves. I think we can all agree that any time a shift is made from say, charging money for God's forgiveness, to a proclamation of justification by grace through faith alone – it is an unequivocally good thing!

What happened during the Reformation on a mass scale was in essence what happens to new believers on an individual level as they encounter deliverance from whatever form of legalism was previously holding them in bondage. Like a drug sent from Heaven, that first dose of freedom has the ability to hook a person for life.

The problem is not that the Reformation failed to reset our course in the right direction for understanding that salvation is by grace alone. It certainly did! The problem was that it could not anticipate and provide answers for the deluge of ongoing *future* attacks and misunderstandings that would inevitably come in subsequent generations. When we insist on reading the Bible *through* tradition, we tend to get locked into one particular era, living in fear of ever questioning whether anything about those assumptions is open to further discussion.

Christianity has a large, global tent and there are a lot of areas and doctrines of secondary importance that we can agree to disagree about. Issues like the meaning and use of spiritual gifts, ideas about eschatology, discussions over the nature of the Lord's Supper or modes of baptism, etc. are things about which we can debate without becoming divisive. But the gospel itself rises to an altogether different level. If there is anything we *must* persist in getting right, it is the gospel. After all, the Apostle Paul claimed that the gospel is the "power of God for salvation of everyone who believes – for the Jew first, and also for the Gentile."[7]

The Need to Raise Questions... and Why it Matters

Before you decide to burn me at the stake for even suggesting these things, allow me to explain what I mean by using modern Calvinism as an example.

Calvinists are those who claim to believe in the essential teachings of the brilliant reformer John Calvin and 500 years worth of his followers. As a qualifier, let me assure you that I am not anti-Calvinist. As someone who pays careful attention to a variety of theological persuasions – I am not unaware of Calvinism's many strengths and its seemingly impenetrable logic.

In this book I am in no way seeking to launch an assault on Calvinism or convince a Calvinist to abandon his or her general perspective. What I *will* do on a few occasions (especially in chapter 3) is call into question a particular way of thinking about the gospel that over the past twenty-plus years has become known as "Lordship Salvation", which I will often refer to using the abbreviation "LS".

This theological perspective is an outgrowth of one of the central tenets of Calvinism – a doctrine known as the *Perseverance of the Saints* (more on that later). At various points I will be raising questions as to whether some of the popular tenets of LS either confuse, dilute or even change the core of the uncut gospel as Jesus and the Apostles presented it.

I was introduced to the teachings of LS when I was a teenager. After a struggling 20-year marriage to my father, my mom had decided it was time to divorce him. A junior in high school at the time, I sided with my dad and began to harbor deep resentment toward my mother for splitting our family apart (at least that's how I saw it at the time).

Overcome with feelings of anger and helplessness about not being able to change her decision to leave, I would rarely waste an opportunity to injure her with my words. At that time I began reading a newly released book which argued very convincingly for a theological view that if someone were *truly* a Christian, he or she by definition would not continue to walk in spiritual defeat or in a seemingly "unrepentant" manner of sin for long periods of time.[8]

Among other things, the book explained that if this *were* the case in the life of a professing believer, then it was questionable as to whether that person was ever truly saved in the first place. This, in a nutshell, is one of the over-arching premises of LS.

Sinking my teeth into these ideas, I now had a theology with which I could justify my angry, hurtful, and self-righteous attitude toward my mother. While I am certain this was never the intention of the authors of the books I was reading, it is an accurate depiction of how the LS message influenced me and many others with whom I have spoken about it since.

For several years, I began to read everything I could get my hands on related to this subject. The message seemed so solid – so biblical! How ridiculous to assume that a person could ever receive Jesus as *Savior* while failing to submit to Him as *Lord*! After all, Jesus called his followers to come and lay down their lives for His cause, didn't He?

As I studied this theological system, my passionate support of these beliefs began to intensify. The more I read, the more convinced I became that this message was true, and the more virulent I was toward those who seemed to be living lives of what I called "compromise".

Throughout this time, I felt as though I was growing leaps and bounds in my understanding of God and Christianity. As I vomited what I was learning onto loads of innocent by-standers, many were kind enough to tolerate my zeal. Some even began to openly affirm my ability to articulate these views, suggesting that I should perhaps "become a pastor someday". It was all going along so perfectly except for just one small detail: there was still a great deal of "compromise" in my life too!

Of course, like any self-righteous fool, this dilemma was easy enough to gloss over when I compared my life the actions of the really "big sinners" I knew. At one point I lived in a nationally known college party town in Northern California. Even though my own lifestyle wasn't anything approaching squeaky-clean, I could always point fingers at the more obvious sinners in order to feel better about myself.

I knew guys who were shacking up with girls every other night, driving home drunk routinely from the clubs, cheating their way through college and then showing up at church on Sunday in search of some way to get forgiven so they could launch a new week of the same regimen. What hypocrites they were! I wasn't even *close* to that sinful.....was I?

Understanding Legalism

It's a funny thing, that little word we call "legalism". We throw the terminology around so often that many Christians don't understand its meaning.

When I was a kid, the old-fashioned people who were resistant to the newer ways of doing things in church were accused of being "legalistic." Likewise, those who had strong beliefs about various social issues like drinking alcohol or viewing R-rated movies were also called "legalists" by other Christians who claimed to be more in touch with exercising their freedoms in Christ. Debating the nuances of old-fashioned social views may be a legitimate topic of discussion, but does it have anything to do with legalism? *Traditionalism*, maybe. *Judgmentalism*, perhaps. But *legalism*?

Legalism – in the biblical sense of the word – is *any attitude or belief that human merit can produce, prove or preserve for oneself an acceptable standing before God.* Read that definition one more time.

> Legalism – in the biblical sense of the word – is *any attitude or belief that human merit can produce, prove or preserve for oneself an acceptable standing before God.*

When I was comparing what seemed like the "lesser" sins of my life with the "greater" sins of others, I was imagining myself to be more spiritual and loveable than them in God's eyes. I would "humbly" and readily admit that I was a sinner, but at least I was not a total hypocrite! After all, when my behavior crossed the line, there was always someone behaving much worse than me, right?

Grading on a Curve and Manipulating the Masses

It is amazing how wonderful we can make ourselves appear when we grade on a curve, comparing our lifestyles to other seemingly more drastic "sinners." And that is only *one* convenient way of wrongly dealing with our guilt and shame.

In Martin Luther's day the Roman Catholic religious-system had for many decades demanded monetary payment in order for people to have their sins forgiven. This practice was known as the selling of *indulgences*. Perhaps even more unthinkable is that folks actually *paid* the fees routinely!

As twisted as this sounds, it highlights just how desperate people can be to feel forgiven – or at least to feel slightly *less* wretched than someone else by comparison! It also serves as a warning about how shamelessly dishonest some religious leaders can become when they attempt to control people by falsifying (however slightly) the uncut message of the gospel.

Today we don't find the literal selling of indulgences as we did prior to the Reformation, but we see similar examples of manipulation in other more subtle forms. Over the centuries legalistic cults and false religions have appeared by the thousands, proving that people will believe almost anything in order to sense the approving embrace of the Divine. What is more amazing is that many of these followers are intelligent people. This is because according to the Bible, deception has little to do with intelligence.

> Over the centuries legalistic cults and false religions have appeared by the thousands, proving that people will believe almost anything in order to sense the approving embrace of the Divine.

The Nature of Deception

From the earliest pages of the Book of Genesis, God paints a picture of Satan as a master deceiver. Adam and Eve were created in the image of God, and prior to sin entering the human race they were as perfect as humans could possibly be.

Presumably, Eve was the most intelligent woman ever to walk the planet. She knew intrinsically how to care for herself, love her husband and tend to her environment. If ever she had a question about anything, she could consult with the very presence of Almighty God who walked alongside of her in the Garden of Eden. But according to Genesis 3, Eve fell into a trap set by Satan – not because she was stupid – but because she was deceived. Lacking in intelligence was not the problem. Lacking in *discernment* was.

Intelligence is linked to knowledge, whereas discernment is a form of spiritual wisdom. Some of the smartest people I know have made some of the most unwise choices you can imagine – and have suffered the highest earthly consequences! So what does this little rabbit trail have to do with a discussion about the essence of the uncut gospel of grace? Quite a lot, actually!

> ... according to Genesis 3, Eve fell into a trap set by Satan – not because she was stupid – but because she was deceived. Lacking in intelligence was not the problem. Lacking in *discernment* was.

Since the gospel of Jesus Christ is the most important and central message of the Bible, then it is reasonable to assume that this message would be subject to the most vicious forms of attack by Satan and his spiritual forces of deception. As I mentioned, Christians can be mistaken about numerous things and still enjoy a strong relationship with God. We can disagree with fellow believers on various matters of opinion and it changes nothing of our eternal standing with the Creator. But if we get the gospel wrong it's a very big deal!

If there is anything that unifies Christians and sets the Way of Jesus and the Apostles apart from other systems of belief, it is the message of *gospel of grace!* But what do we really mean when we use these words and phrases like *grace,* and *free gift*?

Looking Below the Surface

Almost anyone who claims to be a Bible-believing Christian will also claim to agree with the message of grace. They would read or hear the statement that, *"Salvation is by grace through faith"* and eagerly nod in approval. But over the course of time the purity and simplicity of the uncut gospel is prone to be tarnished, edited and watered down by false teaching, misunderstanding and our natural human bent toward legalism.

Legalism seems to be the default-mode of our flesh. We will talk more about the flesh later on, but in essence the flesh is that old pattern of self-reliance in contrast to total dependence upon God. After Adam and Eve were relationally disconnected from God by sin, they tried to "come back" to Him on their own legalistic terms. Genesis 3 paints a rather sad portrait of the first humans attempting to cover their own shame and nakedness in the form of crafting clothing out of fig leaves.

This is legalism in its most raw and vivid form, attempting to make oneself acceptable in the sight of a holy God through human effort. Rather than play that game, God graciously enacted the first recorded blood sacrifice and lovingly covered their shame with the clothing that *He* would provide instead. This was an early hint of things to be revealed in the future sacrificial system, eventually culminating in Christ suffering on the cross as the final sacrifice for sin.

> This is legalism in its most raw and vivid form, attempting to make oneself acceptable in the sight of a holy God through human effort.

Make no mistake about it that I *love* the fact that God used the courage of the Reformers to bring about such a seismic shift in returning the Church to a faith-based rather than works-based understanding of salvation. But the story doesn't automatically end there! Again, Jude 3 reminds every generation to "contend for the faith *once for all entrusted* to the saints".

In part, we contend by asking good questions so as to find out whether our heroes were as "right" as we think they were. Then we can reaffirm what they got right while exposing and opposing the new and ongoing attacks that seek to undermine the purity of the message as Jesus and the Apostles revealed it.

This is what I pray will happen as you read this book, that you will pick up where the Reformers (and all who followed them) left off. Just because a theologian is a persuasive writer or powerful presenter or has a popular media outlet to attract followers who have practically enshrined him or her with "sainthood" does not mean that they should go blindly unquestioned.

The same is true for this book. I don't expect that you will agree with every line in it. Along the way you will read some shocking things because the uncut gospel is a shocking reality. I invite you to wrestle with this book. Sincerely ponder its claims and assertions. Be courageous enough to question your own presuppositions.

If you find that the circles you run with are editing the Gospel in some way, don't automatically bail out on them. First try to affect change from within! Don't become self-righteous or angry. Avoid condescension in your interactions with others. Begin to teach and live by the gospel of grace in such a way that your life itself is the greatest evidence anyone will need in order to be persuaded.

Finally, remember that this book is not intended to be a dry intellectual exercise. It is written from a deeply personal and practical perspective. It is for the faint of heart who routinely struggle with an ever-nagging sense of God's disapproval. It is for the legalists who believe that God will take into account their personal merit (or lack thereof) as a basis for His acceptance. It is for the addicts who wonder if there is any real hope for finding freedom from the domination of sin. It is for those who are disillusioned by what felt like a scam – being told that the gospel was a free gift only to be later informed that there were pages of religious fine print left undisclosed on the contract.

If you feel beaten up or broken down by a religion of rules, requirements and regimens – or if you are trying to minister to those who do suffer in this way – keep reading! Kindred spirits can identify with one another, and you and I both need the ongoing experience of *total freedom* from the myriad of dead religious trappings that seek to ensnare us! May this journey provoke a desire to discover what it means to out-reform the Reformers in contending for the gospel of grace in its raw, uncut form!

Chapter 2: Front-Loaders
(Exposing the False Gospel of Requirements)

I sat there in the coffee shop with Danny, one of the nicest people I had ever met. He was a member of a worldwide religious sect with which he was becoming increasingly disillusioned. According to him, had his spiritual leaders known he was meeting with an Evangelical Christian pastor there would have likely been some small form of hell for him to pay, so he asked me to keep our meeting on the down-low.

I listened intently as he explained the trouble he was having believing that salvation required *nothing* on our part except to receive God's free gift by faith. Armed with a few random Bible verses and some clear indoctrination from his religious background, he wrestled with the possibility that he had been spoon-fed a lie for so long that perhaps he would never be able to grasp the concept of grace.

I gently listened, probed and invited him to keep seeking. As we were wrapping up the conversation he said that he'd like to meet again. He said he felt uncomfortable giving me his phone number in case I called at the "wrong time", so I gave him my contact information and he promised to keep in touch. That was the first and last time I ever spoke with him, but I believe there are millions more like Danny in the world.

Danger at our Doorsteps

Most believers begin to understand early in their relationship with Christ that "good works" do nothing in relation to making a person righteous before God. Yet, cults and pseudo-Christian groups abound claiming that in order to receive salvation, a person must at least "do their best" to live out the ideals of the faith, and only *then* will God "make up the difference" wherever they fall short of perfection.

There are people filling the seats in houses of worship across America who believe in some form of that very thinking. Even in some "Christian" movements, folks profess to live under the New Covenant assurances of grace and yet are persuaded by the notion that unless they combine with grace their efforts to "try harder", it is questionable whether God will accept them.

Bridging the Gap: The Book of Matthew

In the Bible, the Gospel written by the Apostle Matthew provides a beautiful "bridge" between the *prophecies* of the Old Covenant and the *promises* of the New. Its placement as the first book in the New Testament group of Scriptures is beyond genius, for it is one of the most crucial books in understanding the flow of the storyline of grace revealed to us in the Bible.

Imagine further with me the analogy of Matthew's Gospel account as a "bridge" between the Testaments. While being in right relationship with God was always a matter of grace through faith alone and was never initiated or secured through human works, many of the ancient Jews had lost that message under the debris of centuries worth of rebellion, oppression, and convoluted religious teaching.

Having lived under the injustice of foreign empires for several centuries at the time of Matthew's writing, the Hebrew nation had collectively grown frustrated, angry and zealous for the arrival of their long-awaited Messiah. Following a lengthy chain of Gentile occupation dating back to the Assyrians, the Romans were now in power at the time of Christ's birth.

According to historians, the Roman Empire was the most

powerful political giant in history up to that point. In spite of *Pax Romana* (the forced era of relative peace under Roman rule), the realities of unfair tax laws, strong military policing and little concern for the advancement of the Jewish people left the Hebrews desperate and longing for change.

Secular and religious historians agree that prior to the arrival of Jesus Christ, there was an unprecedented Messianic zeal among many Jews. As their prophets had predicted for centuries, they longed for the day when Messiah would emerge as a political ruler who would right every wrong, bring swift vengeance upon Israel's enemies and establish Jerusalem as the capital city of a just and lasting world empire. After all, how else were they supposed to interpret promises about a Messiah that included descriptions of the government resting upon His shoulders and the increase of His power never ceasing?[9]

Like many of us today, however, these Jews were *selective* in their observations of the Scriptures. While it was true that many prophecies pointed to the coming Messiah as a new and everlasting world leader, it was equally true that other prophecies predicted His violent suffering and death.

So which was it? Should the coming Messiah be expected to rule and reign, or to suffer and die? Confused, many of the Jews did the natural thing. They focused on the prophecies they *preferred* to focus on while ignoring or minimizing the parts they didn't care for.

Because of this partial understanding of the mission of Messiah, the first century Jews were waiting for the *Savior* rather than the *Sufferer*. And that is precisely why Matthew begins his Gospel account the way he does. After telling the story of Jesus' birth (chapters 1-2), the author promptly introduces John the Baptist as the forerunner announcing Jesus' public ministry – a prophetic voice of one calling in the wilderness to the Jews, "Prepare the way for the Lord…"

Repenting about Repentance

Most people, whether Christian or not, are familiar with the word "repent". In chapters 3-4 of Matthew both John the Baptist and Jesus emerge with the same simple message: "Repent, for the kingdom of heaven is near" (3:2, 4:17). The term "repent" has probably caused more confusion about the Gospel message than any single word in the New Testament. We will discuss this more in the next chapter, but for now I will drop one of those shockers on you that I promised earlier.

> The term "repent" has probably caused more confusion about the Gospel message than any single word in the New Testament.

Whenever I ask Christians to explain their understanding of the verb "to repent", most will answer with sentiments like "feeling sorry about your sin" or "making a 180-degree turn from sin and toward God" or "confessing and begging God for forgiveness."

Those are the kinds of ideas people typically attach to the word "repentance." And while it is true that some of those ideas may *accompany* repentance, they are a far cry from the actual Biblical meaning of the concept. The Greek verb "to repent" does not mean "to turn from sin" – but rather "to change your mind or perspective."

"What?" you ask. "You can't be serious! What about all the effort I have invested trying to stay 'right with God' or to 'restore fellowship' with Him after I have sinned? What about all the promises I've made to Him about trying harder not to let Him down? Was that all for nothing?"

Let me ask you plainly, what if the answer to that last question was *yes*? What if wallowing in shame, promising you'll do your best to change your behavior and trying really hard to turn your life around have *zero* to do with either being in right relationship with God *or* living a repentant lifestyle? What if all this talk about "dying to yourself" was not only *unhelpful* in your struggle against sin as a Christian, but *unbiblical*?

When John the Baptist and Jesus were proclaiming their message of repentance, the primary focus was not warning people to turn from their sinful lifestyles. By and large, most Jews at the time lived at an outwardly high level of morality – especially by comparison to their Gentile counterparts.

What John and Jesus *were* saying was consistent with exactly what repentance actually means: "Change your mind!" In essence they were saying, "The King is now in your midst, and the Kingdom is imminently available! If you go on expecting the arrival of a political strong-man who will ascend to a throne by force, you're going to miss out on the Messiah altogether! You need to *change your perspective* about what you think Messiah will be like and instead embrace the One who is in your midst, for He is about to reveal Himself publicly as the King you've truly been waiting for!"

But there was a big problem. First century Hebrews didn't want a meek and mild king. They weren't interested in someone born from the womb of a no-named peasant girl from Nazareth! They wanted *the man*! They wanted someone wiser than the Greek philosophers and more powerful than the Roman Caesars.

They wanted the rightful heir to the Hebrew throne - the promised Seed of Abraham and Son of David who would usher in everlasting peace and salvation. Little did they know that Jesus *was* that very man (which is why Matthew begins his Gospel with a genealogy authenticating Christ's family lineage through both Abraham and David).

The question was obvious: Would the Jews – the people of Israel – embrace Jesus as their Christ? New Testament history tells us that a few individuals would, but the nation as a whole would largely reject Him. Toward the end of Matthew 4, Jesus is pictured as calling individuals like Peter and Andrew, James and John, to be His followers. This, again, is the author attempting to convince his original Jewish audience of the reality that Jesus really *was* their King, even exercising His kingly authority to call people to follow after Him.

Matthew further authenticates the legitimacy of Christ's kingly claims by highlighting the fact that He did many miracles to prove He was Divine. And these truths bring us to a crucial point in Matthew's version of the story that ties into the overall message of this book.

Paying Close Attention

As Jesus' popularity began to escalate, large crowds began to follow Him everywhere (Matt. 4:25). At one point, Jesus went up on a hillside and gathered an audience to teach them. This audience was exclusively Jewish, and Christ's message recorded in Matthew 5-7 is known widely as the *Sermon on the Mount.*

Because of its length, beauty and deeply profound content, scholars and theologians have attached to this famous sermon all kinds of fancy nicknames. I've heard preachers describe it with such lofty titles as *The Kingdom Manifesto* or *A Constitution for Christian Living* and so forth.

Those are popular ways in which many believers view this passage, as a set of high standards for Christians to aim for. But I believe those views grossly miss the point. In fact, I sometimes want to chuckle when I hear those descriptions, not because Christ's words fail to mesmerize me, but because in their context they are so much *more* mesmerizing than those descriptions give them credit for!

As with any portion of scripture, the Sermon on the Mount is best understood in its grammatical, historical and literary context. This means that if we are going to interpret the teachings accurately, we must pay careful attention to things such as the use of the original language, the time frame in which the document was penned, and the author's intent in building his arguments using the specific literary genre he has chosen.

As for its genre, Matthew is in the category we would call *historic narrative.* In other words, Matthew is presenting a storyline rooted in the facts of history, with strategic use of various details in order to build a specific argument directed toward a particular audience.

In this case, he is writing to Jews several years after the events of Christ's earthly ministry had transpired. His intent is to convince these Jews that Jesus truly was and is their Messiah. By reminding them of some of the core events of their encounters with Jesus years earlier, Matthew is hopeful they will change their minds (*repent*) about Jesus and place their faith in Him as their resurrected King.

Because "all Scripture is God-breathed"[10] we have to remember that Jesus' words are no more or less the written Word of God than any other portion of Scripture. For some this may come as another shocker, but it is clearly the case. And why is this reality important? Simply because Jesus' words must be interpreted in their proper context just as we would seek to understand any other part of the Bible.

Its Not What You Think

As reverent and majestic as those descriptions may sound, the Sermon on the Mount was not delivered by Jesus to serve as a Christian "constitution" or "manifesto" for Kingdom Living. When Jesus was teaching this message, and when Matthew was placing it in sequence as he built his Gospel narrative directed toward the unbelieving Jews of his day, there was no suggestion whatsoever that these ideals were something anyone could remotely *hope* to live up to. In fact, Jesus' message was quite the opposite!

Congratulations, You're a Failure?

The Sermon on the Mount is a direct confrontation of many of the popular ideas of first century Judaism, some of which were invented and propagated by a group of mostly wealthy and well-educated religious scholars known as the Pharisees. In the Sermon on the Mount (as with many of Christ's teachings), Jesus takes numerous elements of the Mosaic Law and *elevates* them to an impossibly high standard of perfection for his audience to consider. Included among the ideas Jesus communicates in Matthew 5-7 are the following realities:

- If you lust after someone you are guilty of committing adultery
- If you are angry with someone you've murdered them in God's eyes
- If a thief robs you, you are to offer him even *more* than he's already taken

- Always let your yes be "yes" and your no be "no" (perfect integrity)
- Anyone who marries a divorcee commits adultery
- If you don't forgive others, you will not be forgiven by God
- Never worry about anything in life.....ever!

Just a casual glance at these requirements is liable to drive even the most ambitious God-fearer to despair. And that was exactly Jesus' intention! In fact, the key operative phrase in the Sermon on the Mount is given toward the beginning of the message, where Jesus says, "...unless your righteousness *surpasses that of the Pharisees* and the teachers of the law, you will certainly not enter the kingdom of heaven"[11] (emphasis added).

Do you see what Jesus is getting at? The Pharisees were the ones who went to painstaking lengths to ensure they did not violate the Law even in the slightest degree. What Jesus wanted for His listeners to admit was that God's standards of perfection are *so* high, even the most pious among them would fall miserably short of keeping them.

> What Jesus wanted for His listeners to admit was that God's standards of perfection are *so* high, even the most pious among them would fall miserably short of keeping them.

The Wealthy Poor

In Matthew 5:3, at the very beginning of the Sermon on the Mount, Jesus kicks off His message with the words "Blessed are the poor in spirit, for theirs is the kingdom of heaven." That one sentence sets the tone for everything that follows, some of which I have already highlighted.

There were two common Greek words for "poor" that Jesus could have used here. One meant "poor" as in "having much less wealth than average". The other word meant "dirt poor" – literally "destitute" or "bankrupt". This word also carried the idea of having no power, prestige or influence of one's own. It was a term commonly used for beggars. This second term was the word Jesus used in this verse.

Why is this information so relevant to the argument of a book about defining and defending the gospel of grace? The answer is simple. As a bridge between the Old and New Covenant eras, Matthew's historic narrative is contrasting the rules relating to typical *earthly* kinds of kingdoms with the *other-worldly* kingdom Jesus claimed to be offering.

In an ordinary earthly kingdom, for example, winning the favor of the king was usually predicated upon being found "worthy" in his sight and remaining in worthy standing through proper devotion or effort. By contrast the sole requirement for participation in the kingdom Jesus was introducing was not to prove your worthiness, but to admit your *unworthiness*. It began with acknowledging that your only opportunity to attain "worthy" status was by receiving that status as a free gift paid for by the righteous King Himself!

Like the cults and false religions of our day, many of the Pharisees were mixing works with grace in order to foster a greater sense of security and entitlement before God. They were *front-loading* the Gospel, inventing all kinds of preliminary "requirements" in order to make oneself more fit for Divine approval and only *then* trusting that God would "make up the difference."

Jesus repeatedly tried to offer Israel the chance to repent and embrace Him as their Messiah. I believe that whenever He did this, He was offering Israel a legitimate opportunity to experience the fullness of His Messianic kingdom being ushered in right before their very eyes. Theoretically, had the Jews received Him as their long-awaited King, His earthly monarchy could have been established right then and there! In other words, this was God being faithful to offer Israel the Kingdom that He had promised repeatedly through the prophets of ages past. However, from God's sovereign vantage point there was more redemptive work to accomplish in the world.

Continuing through Matthew's Message

Following the Sermon on the Mount, Jesus is pictured as continuing to authenticate His claims through miracles and signs. Matthew soon records the story of his own personal conversion to

Christ (9:9-13), noting that the Pharisees mocked Jesus for daring to associate with "tax collectors and sinners".

Matthew was himself a tax collector – a Jew who worked for the Roman government and was viewed as a traitor by most other Jews. In response to their remarks, Jesus affirmed, "It is not the healthy who need a doctor, but the sick.....I have not come to call the righteous, but sinners".[12]

Do you see what Matthew is trying to establish here as a bridge between the Old and New Testaments? He is trying to make the loudest possible argument for *grace* as the sole qualifying agent between God and man, between the *King* and those who populate the *kingdom*. He is confronting the Pharisaical notion that God will take into consideration a person's hard work or impressive accomplishments when determining His acceptance of them.

In chapter 10 Jesus sends out His twelve core disciples and tells them not to go to the Gentiles, but *only* to the lost sheep of *Israel*. At this point in the narrative He has not yet disclosed God's plans to build a Christian "church" that would be inclusive of Jews *and* Gentiles *apart from* obedience to the Law! That revelation would come a little later in Matthew's storyline.

Over and over Jesus is pleading with the *Jews* to repent, to change their perspective about what they thought their long-awaited King would look like and to receive His grace as their only means of inclusion in the Kingdom. Instead, chapter 12 records the Jewish leaders doing the unthinkable, eventually attributing Jesus' miracles to Satan! This marks a major turning point in the book of Matthew, at which time Jesus begins to focus on revealing a new "form" of the kingdom – a manifestation that would soon take on a very different look.

In Matthew 13 Jesus introduces his readers to the nature of this new form of the kingdom with parabolic illustrations of weeds growing up alongside of wheat, yeast working its way through a batch of dough, treasures hidden in a field, and a fishing net bringing in "all kinds of fish." These parables begin to shed light on the fact that this new form of the kingdom would not be exclusive to Israel and her converts, but would literally consist of a demographic as diverse and intrusive as those word pictures suggest.

Basically, an entity called the "church" would emerge as a body composed of people from *every* race, tribe, tongue and nation of the world! The news that ordinary Gentile "sinners" would be included in the kingdom without any need to embrace Judaic laws and customs was anything *but* music to their Jewish ears. They wanted Gentiles punished – not included!

Finally in Matthew 16, Jesus removes the parabolic veil by revealing His plan to build this "church", an entity against which the gates of hell would never prevail. This new expression of the kingdom – this church – would be comprised of the "whosoevers" who would simply receive the free gift of salvation through trusting in Jesus. In other words, through *belief* alone.

The New Rules for an Upside-Down Kingdom

Are you catching the significance of this? When we pay careful attention to these details, we discover that the entire New Testament is being launched on a very upside-down approach to building a kingdom! It is an approach that is as frustrating to the modern religious establishment as it was to the first century Jews. Consider for a moment the new rules:

1) You do not participate by being found "worthy" in and of yourself
2) You are not required to be an ethnic Jew
3) There are no national boundaries in this Kingdom
4) You *are not* and *cannot* be "good enough" to meet the standards for qualification
5) The King Himself will provide your entrance based on His own merit instead of yours. All you can do to *receive it* is *believe it.*

While this message may sound standard to many Christians, to the first century Jews and especially the Pharisees this was nothing short of scandalous! Jesus was teaching that in order to enter the Kingdom there was just one pesky little requirement: *perfection*. That requirement left them with one of two options: Either find a way to successfully attain to that standard of perfection, or cast themselves wholly upon the grace of Someone who would fulfill the standard on their behalf. That, we shall see, was the central point of the uncut gospel with regard to a person being accepted by a holy God.

Jesus-Plus?

Today many legalistic teachers and movements endorse a "Jesus-plus" message. For them its about "Jesus plus becoming a part of this structure." "Jesus plus adhering to this particular set of tenets." "Jesus plus doing this or that, trying your best and *then* Jesus will make up the difference."

But here is the plain truth: any Gospel that promises Jesus will "make up the difference" is a fraudulent, bootlegged edit and is *not* the gospel uncut. This is because the "difference" between sinful humanity and the Holy God we rebelled against is so vast that no manner of effort can begin to propel a person toward God without falling into the depths of the chasm itself.

Thankfully, many Bible-believing Christians are trained to recognize and reject this front-loading of the Gospel. They will not be easily fooled by the message of those who show up at their front door trying to convince them that they must do certain things in order to receive salvation. But unfortunately, front-loading the Gospel with preliminary *requirements* is no longer the most prevalent attack on the gospel of grace. This we will consider more fully in the next chapter...

Chapter 3: Back-Loaders
(Exposing the False Gospel of Results)

I am almost always amused when I hang out at the mall. If you like to people-watch as my wife and I do, you can have some serious fun without spending a dime!

One of the other things I like to do at the mall is to read misleading advertisements. You should try it the next time you're there. Look for all the ways the retailers try to lure you in, get your attention or sucker you into buying something. One of most common tricks in the world of advertising is the frequent misuse of the term "free".

Not long ago I saw one of these signs at a sports shop that read "Free Gloves...!" As I moved closer toward the sign I was able to see the fine print: "...with purchase of snowboard jacket."

You see it everywhere you go! "Free gift...when you open a credit account." "Free rotation...when you purchase four new tires." "Free car wash...with an eight gallon fill-up". And then there's my all-time favorite: "Buy one...get one *free.*"

Obviously I get the point. Businesses exist to make a profit and these ads help get people in the door. But if we're honest, this is clearly a misrepresentation of the word "free." Gifts are free. Rewards are not.

If I have to *do* something to get a gift other than simply *receive* it, then it's not a gift – it's a reward.

Something is not free if I have "earned" it by agreeing to whatever deed must be done in exchange for the item. Anytime a "free" offer is back-loaded with fine print requiring some aspect of performance-based verification on the part of the recipient, it ceases to be free on that very basis.

In chapter 2 we began to discuss the message of the Book of Matthew. If you were to continue treading through Matthew's narrative, you would encounter one of the most scathing rebukes ever recorded from the mouth of Jesus. According to Jesus the Pharisees were guilty of piling heavy religious demands on people's backs, and for that He fiercely opposed them. Those who tend to envision Jesus as a purely meek and mild Savior, a bit like Mr. Rogers with a beard, would be wise to read Matthew 23 and think again.

Jesus entered into a culture whereby the idea of a relationship with God as a totally free gift – with no fine print attached – was under serious attack. He wasn't afraid to confront these attacks. Sadly, the absolute "freeness" of the gospel of grace is still under assault today, and many aren't saying a word.

The Issues at Hand

So is God's grace *really* free? And what do we mean by the term *free grace* anyway? Admittedly, the phrase is redundant. It is a bit like saying "fast speed" or "close nearness" since by definition, grace *is* totally free! Any alternate understanding would fall miserably short of its Biblical meaning.

In the world of theological debate the term "free grace", which I will hereafter refer to with the abbreviation "FG", was popularized in the 1980's in response to some of the theological positions advanced by various personalities within Evangelical Christianity who espoused the teachings of LS on a popular, mass scale.

While there are some viewpoints within the official *Free Grace* movement that I differ with, I owe a lot to many within its ranks whose teachings helped me break free from the malaise of legalism that once weighted me down. Having said that, from this point forward whenever I refer to "FG" I am not speaking narrowly about the official movement – but about *all* of us who embrace the freeness of God's grace in distinction from a false-gospel that is either front-loaded with miscellaneous requirements or back-loaded with mandatory results.

As I stated in chapter 1, LS is a belief system found mostly among those who see its suppositions as the natural outflow of the Five Points of Calvinism[13] – and especially that of the fifth point: the *Perseverance of the Saints*. Before we go any further, it is necessary to briefly describe some of the core elements of the LS position related to the gospel.

Lordship Salvation – Redefining Terms

On the surface, most LS advocates correctly affirm that personal salvation is received solely by grace through faith in Jesus Christ. At face value this statement accurately reflects Scriptural truth. The major problems with LS however, as with most untrue beliefs, lie below the exposed tip of the iceberg in the way that various terms are understood.

While most Christians are discerning enough to reject an obviously works-based system of salvation (for example, "front-loading" the Gospel as discussed in chapter 2), many fail to understand that the LS view attaches a works-based ideology to the *backside* of the Gospel.

In other words, while Evangelical Christians unanimously reject the notion that human effort can in any way serve as a front-end *requirement* for salvation, many insist that consistent spiritual victory and obvious fruit will always be the inevitable *result* of a true salvation experience. According to LS, without these good works as "proof" a person has little or no right to rest assured of the genuineness of his or her faith in Christ.

Most LS proponents quickly point to James 2:14-26 in defense of their position – a passage where James seems to affirm that real faith will inevitably result in an obvious change of lifestyle. Without this "evidence" of verifiable good works, the claim is made that a person can have no real assurance of salvation.

We will discuss this passage of scripture further in chapter 4, but is that what James is really implying? Is the point of this passage truly about examining whether our works prove our faith to be genuine – or could James be saying something altogether different?

Advocates of FG would question that conclusion, thereby drawing numerous attacks from LS ideologues. It is common for LS proponents to accuse those who disagree with their views of advocating either antinomianism[1] or so- called cheap grace[2] by minimizing the need for "commitment" on the part of the believer.

I will seek to demonstrate that, ironically, the actual "watering down" of the gospel often comes precisely from the theological perspective of LS. This watering down occurs in numerous ways, not the least of which involves a redefining of several key theological ideas found in the New Testament. As I introduced in chapter 2, perhaps the most consequential of this re-definition of terms has to do with the concept of *repentance*.

Questioning the Status Quo

In a message I recently preached at the church where I serve as a pastor, I mentioned that the Greek verb "to repent" does not essentially mean "to turn from sin" or "reform one's lifestyle" as many preachers and teachers have taught for centuries. I explained that this popular definition of repentance is more closely linked to the ancient Roman Catholic idea of *penance* than to a New Covenant understanding of the verb "to repent".

I also affirmed that I too was raised with the idea that repentance means "making a 180-degree turn from sin toward God." In fact, this definition of repentance is so prevalent among Evangelical Christians that it often comes as a shock to people when I question it.

Allow me to further develop this train of thought for a moment

1   total disregard for God's moral standards
2   a phrase borrowed from Dietrich Boenhoeffer to insinuate a "watering down" of the gospel

with you. The Greek verb "to repent" is *metanoeo* - a compound from *meta* (meaning "change") and *gnosis* (meaning "mind, perspective or knowledge"). Etymologically, the definition of the Greek verb "to repent" is clearly *"to change one's mind or perspective."*

The etymology[3] of a biblical word is always the best place to begin our quest to understand its meaning. Once we have identified this, we can begin to consider the various ways in which the word or concept is used scripturally, since context ultimately determines meaning.

The definition of the Greek verb "to repent" is clearly "to change one's mind or perspective." There is no doubt that regret for sin and turning from sin *can and often do* accompany repentance. However, the crucial questions we are seeking to answer are related to whether or not "repentance" and "turning from sin" are in fact synonymous, and whether or not promising to turn from sin is required for forgiveness and salvation.

This may sound like a technicality, but it is *hugely* significant in our understanding of the uncut gospel of grace. Many LS advocates not only define repentance as a heartfelt act of "turning from sin and surrendering to Christ as Master", but also claim that this view of repentance is virtually synonymous with what they call "saving faith."

In contrast, FG advocates will point out that the idea of "turning from sin" as either a *requirement for* or *result of* authentic "saving faith" is actually an inclusion of works as part of the gospel, making Christianity essentially no different from any other legalistic religion.

Many LS advocates get around this critique by their assertion that since God unconditionally "elects" (chooses) those who will be saved, He therefore passes over those whom He has determined will not be saved. In this view, "turning from sin and submitting to Christ as Master" includes nothing of human works since *God* is the One who has unconditionally chosen some to be saved apart from any real freedom of "choice" on their part.

---

3   The study of the true meaning of a word from the root of its linguistic components

In other words, since God essentially "forces" salvation upon His chosen individuals as the evidential work of his own advanced choosing of them, the inevitable "turning from sin" has little or nothing to do with a person's own volition. Instead, it is a sovereignly-imposed work of the Holy Spirit. Hence, this 180-degree turn from sin cannot be considered *works-based* salvation since it is God literally doing all the "work" in causing the person to "turn". Confused yet? Stay with me.

While these ideas raise a whole new set of questions about the fairness and justice of God which will have to be saved for another discussion, the bottom line is that the New Testament word "repent" literally refers to "a change of mind." It goes without saying that it is always desirable for a change of lifestyle to accompany this change of mind. This is why in the very first occurrence of the word in the Book of Matthew, John the Baptist challenges the religious Jews to "produce fruit in keeping with (their) repentance" (Matt. 3:8).

By telling them to "produce fruit", John is addressing a desired change in their lifestyle – and this raises an obvious logical dilemma in this passage: If repentance is *really* synonymous with "changed behavior" (such as turning from sin), then John the Baptist's words are rather redundant since he in essence would be saying *"change your behavior in keeping with your changed behavior."*

Clearly, it seems more reasonable to define repentance by what the word *actually* means rather than read into the term a pre-conceived theological idea that was not originally implied! By this better logic, we can make good sense of what John was saying: "Now change your behavior (fruit) in keeping with your change of perspective (repentance)."

Security vs. Maturity – Which Came First?

A change of lifestyle can (and should) accompany a change of perspective about God and Jesus and life and eternity, but it is unwise to imprecisely use these terms in relation to the gospel. As I have stated previously, Christians can disagree about a lot of things – but if there is anything we *must* strive to be accurate about – it is the uncut gospel of grace!

To put it another way, offering salvation as a free gift based on faith alone while also demanding that true "saving faith" *must* produce a litany of observable evidence (without which you have no right to rest assured you are saved) is essentially a bait-and-switch scam if there ever was one! Whenever our assurance of salvation rests upon our *performance* rather than upon the *promises* of Jesus – we are in big trouble.

If assurance of salvation is impossible apart from any "evidence" beyond simple trust in Christ's finished work, believers have no real hope of experiencing the kind of spiritual growth and security God desires for us. In essence, our *security* is the basis of our *maturity* – not vice versa!

> In essence, our *security* is the basis of our *maturity* – not vice versa!

Resting in God's unconditional free grace toward His children will indeed contribute to that sense of security. However, the LS view cannot make such a claim. At the end of the day, LS can provide little more than a foundation for the kind of morbid introspection and insecurity that commonly precedes spiritual burnout in the lives of so many believers!

Faith and Repentance

When someone exercises faith in Christ (which the Scriptures repeatedly affirm is the sole condition for salvation), that person has *truly* repented. They have *changed their mind* or *perspective* about Jesus. They have gone from *unbelief* to *belief* – from *not trusting* in Christ's finished work of redemption to *trusting in Him alone* as their sole means of rescue.

However, if repentance (erroneously defined as "turning from sin") is indeed a mandatory ingredient for receiving eternal life, the Gospel message is essentially no different from the basic tenets of any other legalistic belief-system whereby one procures or preserves meritorious status before God through supposed outward "proof."

What Must I Do to Be Saved?

When Paul was asked "What must I do to be saved?" he thunderously responded "Believe on the Lord Jesus Christ and you will be saved!"[14]. Jesus and the Apostles were united on this point from start to finish, and we must be also. Of course, this leads to yet another question: "What does it mean to *believe* on Jesus?"

Many ideas have been elaborated on, but in one of the books that greatly influenced my thinking when I formerly held to the LS perspective, the author makes the unfortunate statement that *"True faith is humble, submissive obedience."*[15]

I choose to believe that most who make such claims are not being deliberately dishonest when they write things like this. However, this is at best a gross error in articulating what biblical faith in Christ is. In fairness, these words were later softened in a subsequent revision of the book after being called into question by so many.

Again, the Bible repeatedly affirms that changing one's perspective (repentance) *should be* and *frequently is* a catalyst for the desire to abandon sinful behavior. Often this very change of perspective itself is related to the emptiness of living in sin as opposed to the experience of a fulfilling life in Christ. It is also commanded and desirable that all people, including believers, exercise a lifestyle of repentance (which could include, but not be defined as turning away from a sinful lifestyle through walking by the Spirit rather than the flesh).[16]

The fact is that there are often costly earthly consequences related to living in rebellion against God. For a LS advocate to insinuate that those who espouse the uncut gospel of God's free grace are proponents of *antinomianism* or are unconcerned about personal holiness and godly behavior among believers is simply untrue.

> The fact is that there are often costly earthly consequences related to living in rebellion against God.

Will the Real Gospel Please Stand Up?

With regard to keeping the gospel free from the legalistic focus of either *requirements* (front-loading) or *results* (back-loading), let's briefly summarize the core elements of the uncut gospel of Christ.

While there is a diversity of theological opinion among those who espouse the free grace of God, most from this camp consistently affirm that biblical faith is simply "confidence" or "trust" that the gospel is true on a personal level. This "trust" is a strong personal persuasion that the finished work of Christ on the cross completely satisfied God's righteous anger against sin apart from any supposed "effort" on the front-end of the gospel or so-called "evidence" on the back-end. That Christ's sacrifice completely satisfied and turned away God's wrath against sin is the essential Christian doctrine known as "propitiation".[17]

In the Gospel account written by the Apostle John we find one of the strongest arguments in favor of a FG understanding of the Christian message. The stated purpose of the writing of John's gospel is "that you might *believe* that Jesus is the Christ, the Son of God, and that *by believing you may have life* in his name".[18]

Many statements in the Bible are equally clear that salvation is conditioned upon faith alone in Christ alone,[19] but there is something uniquely remarkable about John 20:31. Again, John 20:31 clarifies John's specific purpose for writing his unique Gospel account – namely, that through simple belief in Christ his readers would receive the free gift of life in Him.

What is so telling here is that the concept of "repentance" is completely absent from the book of John from start to finish. Consequently, even if a person *could* argue that the verb "to repent" means "to turn from sin", it is curiously nowhere to be mentioned in the *one book of the Bible with the most directly stated purpose of leading people to salvation in Christ*!

Not only that, but other "commitment" terms (such as "obey", "submit", etc.) are never used in conjunction with any teaching on receiving salvation or eternal life in John's Gospel. In light of this there are two basic possibilities. Either John presented an incomplete and therefore false version of the gospel message to his readers – or simple faith (trust) in Christ is the only ground for salvation.

Saints or Sinners?

In 1 Corinthians 3, which some LS advocates go to great lengths to dance around a plain reading of, Paul clearly states that the Corinthian believers had *not* yet turned from their sinful ways and were in fact still living "carnal" lives. This was a sad reality for which the Apostle bluntly rebukes them.

If there ever *was* an opportunity for Paul to use the term "repent" to imply a "turning from sin", it would be in this passage. Likewise, if there ever *were* an occasion for Paul to use a person's life-dominating sins as a means of casting doubt on the legitimacy of their salvation, this would be it!

However, in spite of their unfortunate *non-turning-from-sins* state of affairs, Paul repeatedly identifies the Corinthians as genuine Christians. Clearly, these followers had not totally submitted to Christ as "master" of their lives, yet were fully embraced by the Apostle of grace as his spiritual brothers and sisters. We will further discuss this reality later on in chapter 7.

> In the New Covenant letters of Paul, even those struggling with addictive patterns and life-dominating sins were to be viewed according to their true identity in Christ as saints. Never are they referred to as filthy sinners. This is because a person's spiritual identity is a matter of *birth*, not *behavior.*

In his letter to the Romans Paul opens up about a very personal internal battle between the new person he had become in Christ and the flesh that sought to provoke sinful behavior within him.[20] Some commentators feel so uncomfortable about Paul's honesty here that they have devised all kinds of ideas about how Paul certainly must have been referring to his life *prior* to becoming a Christian when he made these statements. You can see how damaging Paul's confession would be to a stringent LS view if simply taken at face value! We will consider this reality more thoroughly in chapter 6.

I could go on, but the point is clear. There is *one* scriptural condition for a sinner to be made right with a holy God: faith in Christ alone. This is the consistent and clear message preached and taught by the Apostles throughout their writings. In the New Covenant letters of Paul, even those struggling with addictive patterns and life-dominating sins were to be viewed according to their true identity in Christ as saints. Never are they referred to as filthy sinners. This is because a person's spiritual identity is a matter of *birth*, not *behavior*. More on that in chapter 11!

What did Jesus mean?

Yet another way in which many LS advocates argue for their position is by highlighting the demanding claims Jesus placed upon His followers as recorded in the Gospel accounts of Matthew, Mark and Luke. While there are certainly legitimate ways to apply many of the words of Jesus to our lives as New Covenant disciples, it bears repeating that we must be extremely careful to interpret His teachings in context.

While the Gospels are wisely organized as the opening books of what we refer to as the *New Testament*, the reality is that the New Covenant itself was not inaugurated until Christ's death and resurrection. Jesus made no mention of its implementation until the night He was betrayed and arrested to be crucified.[21]

The author of Hebrews is abundantly clear that a *will* (testament) does not go into effect until a death has occurred, arguing that this is true in the case of Christ's death inaugurating the New Covenant (Hebrews 9:16-17). Both John and Paul also affirm that Jesus' earthly ministry was implemented among those living under the Law – the Jews.[22]

Technically, Jesus' public ministry took place during a very *transitional* period occurring under the governance of the Old Covenant, also known as the Old System or the Law. Considering this fact is indispensable for accurately interpreting many of Jesus' words recorded in the Gospels.

For example, we have noted that many LS advocates will point to texts such as The Sermon on the Mount (Matthew 5-7) as supposed "proof" of the high demands placed upon Christ's followers. Yet, as we discussed previously, the clear Old Covenant context of the Sermon's placement in both history and in the Book of Matthew cannot be ignored.

It is indeed true that there are many stringent warnings and calls to commitment in the famous Sermon on the Mount, many of which we have already highlighted. These include: *lust being equated with adultery, hatred being equal to murder, the need to be more righteous than the most pious religious people in history,* and *the warning that we will be judged in the same way we judge others.*

We have already established that the main point of the Sermon on the Mount, taken in context with the overall argument of Matthew, has little if anything to do with calling Christians to a greater degree of commitment. The words were spoken to Jews who were struggling with the ever-increasing problem of legalism and self-righteousness.

By elevating the Law of God to an even *more* stringent standard than His audience had previously understood it, Jesus was essentially pointing out that in and of ourselves, *meeting God's perfect standards is impossible!*

Putting the Law in its Place

When people attempt to share the Gospel today, some use the Law of God as a way to help unbelievers comprehend that they are sinners by nature and by choice. If done gently and in the proper context, asking a non-believer if they have ever lied, lusted or stolen can be a helpful way to illustrate that *all* humans are born with a common bondage to sin until Christ sets us free.

In similar fashion, Jesus' Sermon on the Mount confronts a universal, legalistic mentality by illustrating that even on our very best days, nobody is righteous enough to please God based on his or her own merits. There are many other examples of how various bootlegged versions of the Gospel misrepresent the context of Christ's teachings in order to defend erroneous views.

Unfortunately, the LS view of grace scratches an itch for us, appealing to the baseline legalism of our flesh. By attaching mandatory works to the *backside* of Gospel like fine print disguised on a contract for the unsuspecting customer to conveniently discover *after* the fact, LS actually becomes the perspective which in fact "waters down" the gospel and the meaning of grace.

In a strange twist of irony, those who accuse the FG position of advocating "cheap grace" actually diminish the value of real grace by destroying the very quality that makes the gospel what it is: a no-strings-attached free gift of selfless love and salvation from a loving Heavenly Father.

It goes without saying that there are appropriate ways to apply the pre-cross teachings of Jesus to our lives as Christians, including much of the content of the Sermon on the Mount. But legitimate *application* can only occur once an accurate *interpretation* is arrived at.

Are the basic ideals represented in the Sermon on the Mount desirable qualities for followers of Jesus? Certainly they are! Were they preached by Jesus as a *Constitution for Christian Living*? Don't kid yourself! Rather, these demands embody a declaration intended to drive the Pharisee in *all* of us to the desperate realization that we need the grace of God *alone* to provide our righteousness!

As many LS proponents lament, the gospel is definitely being compromised these days, but ironically the views of LS are some of its principle compromises. Sadly, many adherents of LS don't understand what they are believing or advocating. This is why we must remember that the gospel of grace is not a peripheral issue. It is *the* issue, and it is worth passionately contending for. After all, if we get this wrong... nothing else matters.

Chapter 4: God in the Hands of Angry Sinners?

Surfing Youtube is a fantastic way to waste time. Like me, you probably have at least a mental list of some of your top videos. Some of the my favorites are when I discover that a person has edited a political speech – such as the State of the Union Address – in order to make the President say something he didn't say.

Stringing unrelated phrases together for the purpose of comedy may be fun and harmless when you're posting it on Youtube for a few laughs. It's not so funny, however, when we do essentially the same thing with the Bible.

Unfortunately, preachers do it all the time, stringing unrelated Biblical phrases together for the purpose of supporting their point of view. I'm not saying that every one of these preachers is grossly misleading their audience by doing so, but it is a very dangerous way to teach the Bible – especially in the hands of the wrong leader.

Often preachers teach on specific phrases or verses in order to support their own angry, distorted projections of God. Some have blatantly turned God into an irritable tyrant while others have shifted the truth more subtly with deceptive double-talk and cliché-ridden assumptions that are not really grounded in truth. This is why it is important for Christians to read the Bible for themselves instead of blindly trusting an individual or group to lead them.

When discussing such important matters as God's grace and His gospel, it is not unusual for the mind to drift in the direction of "Yes, but what about that one verse...?" Those are precisely the right kinds of questions to ask! If the gospel truly *is* about an unconditional free offer of forgiveness and being brought into the abundant life of God through no effort of your own – and if there is nothing good *or* bad you can do to make God accept you more or less than He does at the moment of salvation – then what about those famous so-called "warning passages"?

Once Again, Context is Everything

The great news about the Bible is that it is *not* a list of random sound-bites, pithy quotes or disjointed pearls of wisdom. Rather, it is an unfolding storyline filled with human personality, unexpected twists and turns, and a given literary, historic and grammatical context in which every word is written.

In a world of email, text-messaging and social networking, we have all been the victim of having our words taken out of context, and we hate it when it happens! One of the realities of our fallen world is that we suffer from an environment prone to miscommunication and its consequences. And while God understands this, I am certain He does not enjoy having *His* words taken out of context any more than we do!

The Bible proclaims itself to be the written word of God – and "profitable" for a variety of practical purposes.[23] Yet as powerful as the Scriptures are – and as dynamic as the Holy Spirit is to help us in our understanding – we cannot simply approach the Bible as a list of mystical proof-texts waiting to back up our opinions and ideas.

We are still humans requiring diligence in our pursuit of understanding the words of Scripture in their proper context if we are going to arrive at accurate conclusions. Too many angry preachers have molded God into their own image for their own purposes of controlling and manipulating people and airing their own opinions.

I have known many who defend the idea that a person's assurance of salvation involves either *requirements* or *results* as part of the equation. And while I cannot possibly cover every phrase or statement in the Bible that one might submit as "proof" of those perspectives, almost without exception there are three passages that are commonly brought to the forefront to advance this distorted vision of the gospel. In what follows, we will deal with them one at a time, attempting to set them in an accurate context so as to shed greater light on their meaning.

> Too many angry preachers have molded God into their own image for their own purposes of controlling and manipulating people and airing their own opinions.

Romans 14:10 – Christians Facing Judgment?

Toward the end of his letter to the early Roman church, Paul alerted the believers to a startling reality: *"we will all stand before God's judgment seat"*. He also told the Corinthian believers that "we must all appear before the judgment seat of Christ, that each one may receive what is due him for the things done while in the body, whether good or bad" (2 Cor. 5:10).

So what's the deal? If Christ has promised those who believe in Him that they will *not* suffer God's wrath, condemnation or judgment, then why are these statements, spoken about Christians, included in the New Testament?

At first glance, this language seems to stand in stark contrast to Paul's teaching about salvation being by grace through faith and not of works. Paul repeatedly affirms throughout his writings that salvation cannot in any way be earned, merited, proven or secured through human works. And yet in this passage, he says that each of us will in some way receive that which is "due" to us for our works. Is Paul contradicting himself? As I will seek to demonstrate, the answer is no…

The Meaning of the "Judgment Seat"

When referring to this so-called "judgment seat" that Christians will face after passing on from this life, Paul uses a very specific Greek term: *Bema*. A Bema was a raised platform upon which "judges" would sit in ancient times, whose job it was to evaluate the contestants and declare the winners of various Olympic-style contests in the Greco-Roman world. The winners of various competitions at the Isthmian Games, for example, were "rewarded" by the judges who sat upon this *bema* platform for their excellence in completing and winning a race or competition.

It is important to distinguish the Bema from the wrathful judgment that God will pour out against those who have rejected His salvation. There is nothing wrathful or punitive involved in the Bema. If we are to take Paul's analogy at face value, it is presented as a place of celebration where believers will in some way be recognized for allowing God to use them in the building of His kingdom enterprise during their lives on earth.

While the Greek word *bema* is used in the Gospels and Acts to refer to the raised platforms where various Roman magistrates would make decisions (Matt. 27:19; John 19:13), Paul's use of the word was likely related to its original use among the Greeks as indicated by his frequent analogies to the Christian life being like a "race" with a prize to be won.[24]

In its cultural context then, the Bema is a "reward seat" only and portrays a time where those who have run the race will be given some kind of recognition. It is not, however, a place where believers are judged for their sins. Judgment for our sins has already been taken out on Jesus Christ in our place, and we will never incur God's wrathful judgment in either this life or the next (John 3:18; 5:24; 6:37; Rom. 5:1, 9; 8:1; 1 Cor. 11:32; 1 Thess. 5:9).

Many people hear about the *Judgment Seat of Christ* and nervously wonder whether this will be a time when a videotape of all their past sins and failures will be played for the world to see. The answer is unequivocally "no"! That tape no longer exists!

Paul elsewhere told the Corinthians that this would be an event where all of our works which prove *valuable* to the kingdom will survive and be recognized, while our works which prove to be *worthless* to the kingdom will be "burned up" (1 Cor. 3:10-15). This of course is consistent with God's promise to "remember our sins no more" (Jer. 31:34; Heb. 10:17).

We must not forget that at the Bema, our *works* are being "judged" or evaluated, but not *we ourselves*! In addition, if our worthless works are burned up and remembered no more, the focus will only be upon the fruit born in our lives through the power of the Holy Spirit living the life of Jesus through us. So in reality, when we receive this "reward" at the Bema, Jesus receives the glory anyway!

> Many people hear about the *Judgment Seat of Christ* and nervously wonder whether this will be a time when a videotape of all their past sins and failures will be played for the world to see. The answer is unequivocally "no"! That tape no longer exists!

When Will the Bema Occur?

Apparently this time will occur just following the Rapture or Resurrection of believers after we are "caught up together to meet the Lord in the air" (1 Thess. 4:13-18). Keathley explains a brief overview of support for this idea:

> (1) In Luke 14:12-14, reward is associated with the resurrection and the rapture is when the church is resurrected.
>
> (2) In Revelation 19:8, when the Lord returns with His bride at the end of the tribulation, she is seen already rewarded. Her reward is described as fine linen, the righteous acts of the saints—undoubtedly the result of rewards.
>
> (3) In 2 Timothy 4:8 and 1 Corinthians 4:5, rewards are associated with "that day" and with the Lord's coming. Again, for the church this means the event of 1 Thessalonians 4:13-18.
>
> So the order of events will be (a) the rapture which includes our glorification or resurrection bodies, (b) exaltation into

the heavens with the Lord, (c) examination before the *Bema*, and (d) compensation or rewards. [25]

Who Will Be Involved in the Bema Experience?

As noted earlier, Paul said that "all" believers would appear before the Bema (2 Cor. 5:10). Every New Testament passage dealing with the Bema or the receiving of a crown or reward seems to be directed toward *believers only*. Again, the emphasis is on celebrating the fruit of Christ's work in our lives – not on being "saved" from hell or judgment against our sin (Rom. 14:10-12; 1 Cor. 3:12ff; 2 Cor. 5:9ff; 1 John 2:28; 1 Thess. 2:19-20; 1 Tim. 6:18-19; Tit. 2:12-14). Salvation from God's wrath against our sin is a free gift based on grace through faith alone (Ephesians 2:8-9; 1 Thess. 5:9-10).

The Practical Impact of the Bema

Obviously, the New Testament writers did not include these teachings about the *bema* in order to fill our minds with pointless information. There are very practical reasons for our belief in the future reward of those who run the race faithfully in this life by the power of the Spirit of Christ.

Some have suggested that the idea of rewards for faithful believers diminishes grace or impugns the idea of serving Christ out of a motive of pure love for others and glory given to Him. But this simply isn't the case. If anything, the doctrine of rewards further *distinguishes* grace from works and *encourages* us to live for His glory and the love of others!

Choosing to live in rebellion against God can and often does result in terrible consequences. These consequences are not related to whether we will go to heaven when we die, but they are nonetheless important motivating factors in our lives. Some of the obvious potential consequences of choosing to live in rebellion against God include:

1) *Natural consequences.* It is a well-established fact that a person "reaps what he sows" (Gal. 6:7). This does not mean that we

will always suffer to the extent we may deserve, nor does it imply that making good choices will always protect us against suffering. It simply means that generally speaking over time, a person whose lifestyle is honoring to the Lord will reap something good. The Book of Proverbs makes this abundantly clear. In fact, a person does not necessarily have to be a Christian to see the reality of reaping and sowing at work in his or her life.

2) *Divine Consequences.* We understand from Scripture that there is a stark contrast between God's wrathful punishment (which believers are now exempt from by grace through faith in Christ) and His loving discipline as a Heavenly Father. Like any good father, God will discipline His children, even *proving* by His discipline that He truly does love us enough to bring correction to our lives (Heb. 12:5-11). We must keep in mind that God's discipline is about helping us become "disciples" of Jesus after we are saved, and not about rubbing our nose in our mistakes and sins.

3) *Personal Consequences.* When we live in stubborn rebellion against God, there are also potential personal consequences, such as the existential feelings of guilt upon our conscience and the damage to our interpersonal relationships that often results from the wreckage of careless living. We open ourselves up more to the brutal attacks of Satan as he seeks to accuse us and paralyze us from serving fruitfully due to feelings of hypocrisy and defeat. Living in secret rebellion can also take a physical toll, even bringing sickness or disease to our body through the internal stress and torment of it all (Psalm 32:3-5; Prov. 17:22; 14:30 1 Cor. 11:29-30; 1 John 5:16-17).

4) *Eternal Consequences.* The *bema* is just as consequential as any of these other areas for motivating us to grow in the grace

and knowledge of Jesus. The Bible doesn't go into great detail about what these rewards will look like or what form they will take, but they are apparently part of a grand celebration for the Body of Christ in the future and are something we can be motivated by without feeling selfish, but rather *grateful*.

Is the Doctrine of Future Reward Really Taught Throughout the New Testament?

It is the experience of many Christians – after receiving initial teaching about the *bema* – to ask themselves "How could I have possibly missed this? Is this concept *really* taught in the New Testament, or is this just a random couple of statements by Paul which we might be misinterpreting?" You can judge for yourself by considering the following small sampling from the New Testament. Among other things...

1. Believers are promised various "crowns" in relation to the fruit of their lives (1 Cor. 9:25; 2 Tim. 4:8; James 1:12)

2. Jesus and the Apostles talked about storing up treasure in Heaven based upon faithfulness to Christ and His teachings (Matt. 6:20; 1 Pet. 1:4)

3. The promise of being told "Well done, good and faithful servant" (Matt. 25:21; Lk. 19:17; 1 Cor. 4:5b) is somehow related to how believers live.

4. Special promises are given to those believers who are described as "overcomers" (Rev. 2:7; 2:11, 17, 26)

5. The promise of special responsibility and authority in the future Kingdom is given based upon faithfulness (Matt. 19:28; 24:45-47; 25:21, 23; Lk. 19:17-19; 22:29-30; Rev. 2:26)

Have you ever wondered why Jesus would say something like *"great is your reward in Heaven"*? Or have you pondered Jesus' statements about some people being called "great" in the kingdom while others will be called "least"? How could these things be true when we are all equally saved by grace alone? The often-ignored issue of the *bema* of Christ is hugely significant in helping us understand these apparent contradictions.

Salvation is *not* a reward. Neither is it a loan, a bribe or a paycheck. It is a *free gift* that can be *freely received* simply by believing in the finished work of Jesus dying in our place and rising from the dead. *"Believe on the Lord Jesus Christ and you will be saved"* – period, end of story! (Acts 16:31).

However, don't allow that glorious reality to lead you to believe that the way you live your life is unimportant or inconsequential now that you're *in grace*. After Paul passionately defended the uncut gospel of God's free grace to the Galatians, he said to them "The only thing that 'counts' is faith expressing itself through love" (Gal. 5:6).

In what sense was he saying that our faithful expressions of love 'count' for anything? Did he mean that our works of love 'count' toward earning (or "proving") our salvation? Absolutely not! Rather, he was mindful of the future reward available to those who – motivated by love rather than legalism – allow the Lord to live His supernatural life through them!

James 2:14-26 – A Litmus Test for Legitimacy?

James 2 has long been a key operative text in attempting to legitimize the idea that all true Christians will inevitably "verify" they are truly saved by their litany of outward good works. Well-meaning believers have for centuries pointed to this passage as evidence for some version of LS – the idea that one cannot receive Jesus as Savior without also submitting to Him as Master (thereby "proving their salvation" with mandatory, observable results in the realm of good works). The key statements from James 2 which lead to that conclusion are found in verses 14-26 as follows:

"(14) What good is it, my brothers, if a man *claims to have faith but has no deeds*? Can such a faith save him?...(17) In the same way, *faith by itself, if it is not accompanied by action, is dead...*(19) You believe that there is one God. Good! Even the demons believe that – and shudder...(21) Was not our ancestor Abraham *considered righteous for what he did* when he offered Isaac on the altar?...(24) You see that a person is *justified by what he does and not by faith alone*. (25) In the same way, was not even Rahab the prostitute *considered righteous for what she did* when she gave lodging to the spies and sent them off in a different direction? (26) *As the body without the spirit is dead, so faith without deeds is dead.*"

Admittedly, these are some strong statements that at first seem to stand in contradiction to an abundance of clear Biblical promises about salvation being available only by grace through faith (including John 3:16, Romans 3:28, Romans 4:5, Galatians 3:1-3, Ephesians 2:8-9 and dozens of others). The potential for confusion is so strong that Martin Luther actually wanted the letter of James to be eliminated from the New Testament!

In an effort to reconcile this apparent contradiction between James and Paul, theologians have attempted every imaginable manner of mental gymnastics. The most popular idea among those from Reformed and Evangelical persuasions claims that James is teaching that outward "deeds" are the necessary evidence in assuring others and ourselves that our faith in Christ is genuine rather than phony. This is a dominant teaching of LS theology. But is this really what the passage is saying?

While there is some variance among those who interpret this text in light of the uncut gospel, what we all agree on is that James's words *cannot* mean that the life of *every* single true believer will be characterized by a litmus test of "good works". For a better understanding of this passage, I invite you to consider the following realities...

Three Huge Questions

In considering the context of James' words, we must ask three significant questions: 1) What does James mean by his use of the word *save*?, 2) What does James mean by his use of the word *dead*? and 3) In what sense does James handle the concept of *justification*? A simple look at the overall argument of the letter is indispensable for us here.

James uses the term "save" on five different occasions in his letter, initially in 1:21, where he writes

> "Therefore, putting aside all filthiness and *all* that remains of wickedness, in humility receive the word implanted, which is able to save your souls" (NASB).

It is crucial to note that at this point in the letter James is clearly addressing those who are *already* genuine believers in Jesus Christ. He repeatedly refers to his audience with such terms as *brothers, beloved, believers in our glorious Lord Jesus Christ, righteous, etc.* – all descriptions which only apply to those he is confident are saved. Additionally, he speaks to them as those who are having their "faith tested" by trials (1:2-4). This kind of language can likewise only apply to someone whom the author assumes is a genuine Christian.

So if James is speaking to those who are already "saved" in the eternal sense – that is, they have been rescued from judgment and forgiven of their sins through faith in Christ – then his use of the word "save" in 1:21 cannot be used in that same sense. Because this word "save" is used in terms of something that *can* or *is able to* happen rather than as something that has *already* happened, James is apparently speaking about an aspect of salvation *other than* that of receiving eternal life by grace through faith.

Now add to this reality the fact that James stated earlier in 1:14 that "...sin, when it is full-grown, gives birth to death." It is important to understand that the book of James is not an evangelistic book seeking to educate people about the essence of so-called "saving faith." Rather, it is an admonishment to *Christians* about the futility of persisting in sin, affirming that "sin...gives birth to death" – that is, physical death, death to relationships, death to peace of mind, death to the opportunity of a more fulfilling life, etc. He sets his entire letter up along the lines of practical living, not eternal life.

Having established this contextual foundation, we can move into the latter part of chapter 2 with a better understanding of James' crucial question: "What good is it, my brothers, if a man claims to have faith but has no deeds? *Can such faith save him?*"

Contextually, James is not suggesting that his audience use the presence of good deeds in their lives as a litmus test for determining whether they are genuine Christians! He is using "save" in the same sense in which he has earlier introduced it – as something practical that can *rescue* or *spare* a person from the deathly physical, relational and emotional consequences associated with living in rebellion against the Source of abundant life!

The fact is that no one – whether Christian or otherwise – will experience a fulfilling life when living principally to gratify their own hedonistic desires. The pursuit of selfishness always ends in emptiness – futility – and how much *more* tragic for the Christian who has the opportunity to walk by the Spirit!

> The pursuit of selfishness always ends in emptiness – futility – and how much *more* tragic for the Christian who has the opportunity to walk by the Spirit!

This sheds light on James' use of the word *dead* also. He says three times that faith without works is "dead". To understand his usage, we must look no further than the immediate passage. In 1:15, he gives a hypothetical scenario. "Suppose a brother or sister is without clothes and daily food. If one of you says to him, 'Go, I wish you well; keep warm and well fed,' but does nothing about his physical needs, what *good* is it?" The word translated "good" in the NIV is the Greek word for "profit". He is literally asking *"what profit is this kind of faith?"*

The preceding context points to the fact that *dead* faith means *profitless* faith in terms of practical impact. It does not suggest "phony" or "non-existent" faith, as the LS position insists. In James 2:20, he confirms this analysis with the statement, "You foolish man, do you want evidence that faith without deeds is *useless*?" Again, *useless* is a synonym for *profitless*.

Furthermore, James illustrates his intentions when he writes, "As the body without the spirit is dead, so faith without deeds is dead" (2:26). No one would suggest that a dead body is a phony or non-existent body. Rather a dead body is a real body that lacks *vitality*. It is "profitless" or "useless" for making any practical impact in the world, as is clearly seen in the context of James' argument.

Finally, the statements in this passage that typically cause the most confusion are related to the issue of *justification*. Some critics will accuse Paul and James of contradiction based on this passage. By way of review, Paul's teaching on justification is about God the Judge "ruling in our favor" – declaring us to be righteous based on faith in Jesus alone apart from any works of the law (Rom. 3:21-25; 4:1-5; Gal. 3:1-14, etc.).

Meanwhile, James says the following in chapter 2 of his letter: "Was not our ancestor Abraham *considered righteous* (justified) for what he did when he offered his son Isaac on the altar? (verse 21). And again in verses 23-24, he adds, "And the scripture was fulfilled that says, 'Abraham believed God, and it was *credited to him* as righteousness,' and he was called God's friend. You see that a person is justified by what he does and *not by faith alone*."

Lifted out of context, it is no wonder skeptics point to these words as a blatant contradiction of Paul's New Covenant teaching! Yet, both Paul and James appeal to the same Old Testament verse – Genesis 15:6 – in making their point.

Paul says in Romans 4:2-3, "If, in fact, Abraham was justified by works, he had something to boast about – *but not before God*. What does the Scripture say? 'Abraham believed God, and it was credited to him as righteousness.'" (emphasis added).

By their joint appeal to Genesis 15:6, both Paul and James affirm that they understand the doctrine of imputed righteousness before God – that being in "right standing" with God comes through belief (faith) alone. What James does in the context of the practical focus of his book is to introduce a *second type of justification*. This second type of justification has nothing to do with a Christian's imputed righteousness before God, but rather, with practical righteousness before men.

In spite of his fame, Abraham made many mistakes, several of which glare at us from the pages of Genesis. Clearly James' readers knew this and were aware that God had declared Abraham to be righteous by faith (Genesis 15) long before he ever offered Isaac on the altar (Genesis 22).

> Abraham's obedience *neither initiated nor proved* the reality of His righteous standing with God. That reality was assured by God's promise alone.

Abraham's obedience *neither initiated nor proved* the reality of His righteous standing with God. That reality was assured by God's promise alone. What Abraham's obedience *did* accomplish was to show that his faith was not "useless". It showed that his faith was "made complete" (James 2:22). The word "complete" literally means "mature".

A maturing faith is the exact opposite of a useless, unprofitable faith. It is a faith that is actively involved in showing the world something of who God is. It is a faith that is growing in the abundant life Jesus offers. And while James points to this as an impetus for his audience to live out their faith in tangible ways, he would be horrified to know that many centuries later Christians were using his words to insinuate a litmus test for the so-called "legitimacy" of faith in a believer's life!

Two Kinds of Faith?

Advocates of LS routinely contrast the fictitious terms "saving faith" with "non-saving faith", insinuating that James is talking about two kinds of faith here. But when we understand his terminology in its context, we find that the issue is not really about two kinds of faith, but *two kinds of justification*!

One kind is justification before *God* which only He sees and which is by faith alone. The other kind is justification before our fellow *man*

– which can be observed, which is accomplished through works of love and which can "save" a person from the earthly consequences of selfish living up to and including the death he warned about in 1:15.

Simply put, having basic orthodox beliefs about Christ, while a crucial part of what it means to trust Him for *eternal* life, cannot "save" you from the earthly consequences of sin in *this* life. Only obedience to Christ will enable a person to experience the kind of fulfillment God offers in this life to anyone who abides in Him as a response to His lavish grace.

The sole qualifying factor for our justification before God is faith (i.e. trust) in Christ's sacrificial death and resurrection. When a person exercises this trust, he or she is irreversibly adopted into God's family and is eternally secure in that relationship (Romans 8:38-39). The Bible makes no such distinction between so-called "saving faith" and "non-saving faith".

Scripture does not delineate between "head" Christians and "heart" Christians. This is another reality we glean from the Gospel of John, in which every time the word "faith" is used, it is in reference to "saving" faith. When it comes to faith in Jesus Christ, there is no other kind of faith – period. If it were not for this solitary passage in James 2 being so grossly misunderstood, such a dichotomy would likely never have been inserted into the realm of Christian theology.

The Faith of Demons

Another fallacy advanced by proponents of LS concerns James' mention of the faith of demons. Earlier we noted that part of James' argument is stated as follows in James 2:19: *"You believe that there is one God. Good! Even the demons believe that – and shudder."*

Many will claim that the purpose of these words are to compare and contrast this so-called "saving faith" with "non-saving faith" – which basically amounts to "mere intellectual assent" to a set of facts, according to LS.[26] But this line of reason falls short in a variety of ways.

For starters, the demons' so-called "faith" in God is clearly not faith in the gospel, since it is merely an affirmation of monotheism (belief in one God). Nowhere in the Bible is it suggested that monotheism is equal to the faith through which humans receive salvation. Many people believe in God (just like the demons) yet are not saved since they refuse to trust in Christ alone and His finished work of redemption. This is another affirmation that eternal life is not in view here.

The argument breaks down even further when we consider that demons cannot be saved in the first place. The New Testament repeatedly affirms that the fate of demons is already sealed (Matt. 8:29; 25:41; Jude 6), so it is highly unlikely that the author would use demons as a hypothetical element to his argument if indeed he were talking about receiving eternal life. What this text does show is that faith is faith – period. If anything, the emphasis is not placed upon different *kinds* of faith, but different *objects* upon which faith can be placed: monotheism versus trust in Christ.

Additionally, if the author is indeed arguing that good works are a litmus test for true assurance of salvation, it is a curious reality that Satan and his demons actually have the power to perform countless good works in order to deceive people. If outward works are a litmus test for assurance, then perhaps we should presume that Satan and his demons *are* in fact saved, since they are able to perform counterfeit signs and wonders (2 Thess. 2:9-11).

In fact, we might also be persuaded to believe that members of various pseudo-Christian cults should also rest assured of *their* salvation based on their high quantity of visible "good works." Ironically, many people from legalistic cults *do in fact* believe they are saved, viewing their good works as both a requirement *and* result in proving it.

The essential reality remains that which has already been stated. Whenever our assurance of salvation rests upon our *performance* rather than upon the *promises* of the Gospel of grace alone, we are setting ourselves up for an experience of the Christian life that is contrary to the confidence and security that God intends for us to enjoy. As Dr. Charles Bing rightly observes,

James 2:19 should not be used to argue that works are needed to prove saving faith. This verse shows that demons have a real faith. They believe in one God and know that God has sealed their fate in judgment, therefore they tremble. But they do not and cannot believe in Jesus Christ as their Savior. While good works are God's purpose for us...they cannot prove or disprove the reality of saving faith. Eternal salvation is by grace alone through faith alone—apart from any works at any time.[27]

Are There Any Other Views?

In his must-read book *The Naked Gospel*, pastor and author Andrew Farley brings another angle to interpreting this controversial passage. I include his view here to demonstrate that even if a person is skeptical of the contextual arguments I have just presented, there are other solid ways to view what James is saying without affirming the erroneous LS view.

Farley contends that James is *indeed* talking about salvation from sin leading to eternal life in this passage – and has no problem with James's assertion that we are saved by works and not by faith alone. The key, he argues, is in understanding what James means by "works". He explains...

> "Rather than assuming that *works* should be understood as a lifelong record of religious activity, one should consult the biblical text and let the writer himself define the term. James's own use of the term "works" is quite different from how we use it today."[28]

We will get back to Farley's thought in a moment, but here it is interesting to note that only a few verses later, James acknowledges that "we all stumble in many ways." (James 3:2). James seems to be agreeing with Paul's confession in Romans 7, that there were behaviors in his life (and every believer's life) that in many ways seem to contradict the desire to follow Jesus with whole-hearted consistency. In fact, the entire book of James is a call to live a righteous life, practically speaking – while acknowledging that we routinely fall short in and of ourselves.

If "obedience to Jesus as Master" is the automatic disposition of those whose faith can be said to be "genuine", then must ask why James (or Peter, Paul, John, etc.) would have spent so much energy seeking to *correct* the sinful and selfish behaviors and attitudes of genuine believers in their letters. Clearly, LS misses the mark in its assertion that the truly saved will *always* live in a trajectory of increasing victory over sin throughout their experience in this life.

Also, if "surrender to Christ as Master" is required for salvation, another series of questions arises. How surrendered is surrendered? Is it enough to be fifty percent surrendered? How about seventy-five percent? Will ninety-nine percent do the trick? At what point are we able to discern what God accepts as surrender to Christ's lordship? Obviously nobody lives in a state of one hundred percent conscious surrender to Christ as master or we would never sin!

But now back to James 2 and the issue of James' use of the word "works". Dr. Farley goes on to explain his belief that by using Abraham (and also Rahab) as illustrative of genuine faith, James is making the point that they "actively responded to God's message." He elaborates,

> They didn't sit back passively and claim that they believed God. Rahab decided to open her door to the spies (Joshua 2:1), and Abraham chose to offer his son on the altar (Genesis 22:3). They went beyond mere intellectual assent and did something in response to God's message. But how many times did Rahab open the door? Once. And how many times did Abraham hoist his son Isaac to the altar? Once. Hence, works in this passage is really *not* about a lifelong track record of good behavior. It's actually about the importance of responding to truth – an act that goes beyond intellectual agreement.[29]

While Farley's thoughts on James 2 are unique from mine, I

include his perspective here to illustrate that even those who affirm the view that James *is* in fact talking about faith in relation to eternal life can also remain true to the reality that James is not and *cannot* be demanding that works are a litmus test in determining whether a person's faith is genuine. Simply put, works *may be* an indicator of genuine faith, but using James to prove that they *must be* goes beyond the scope of the uncut gospel of salvation by grace through faith alone.

Hebrews 10:26-39 – Losing our Salvation?

While James 2 is the classic passage many use to defend the idea that good works must *prove* the legitimacy of our salvation (back-loading the Gospel with mandatory results), Hebrews 10 is often used to suggest that believers can *lose* their salvation by falling into repeated sin. Some of the statements from Hebrews 10 which seem to point in that direction include:

> If we *deliberately keep on sinning* after we have received the knowledge of the truth, *no sacrifice for sins* is left, but only a *fearful expectation of judgment* and of raging fire that will consume the enemies of God.[30]

Once more, context is literally *everything* in the pursuit of accurately determining the author's intent. Can I possibly beat this drum any louder? It is critical to note that the author of Hebrews sets up the entire argument of the letter upon the following premise:

> The Son is the radiance of God's glory and the exact representation of his being, sustaining all things by his powerful word. After he (Jesus) had provided purification for sins, he sat down at the right hand of the Majesty in heaven.[31].

The significance of the phrase "he sat down" simply cannot be overstated. It is repeated numerous times throughout Hebrews for emphasis, including here in Chapter 10. More than anything, Hebrews presents Jesus in His role as our ultimate and final High Priest.

Under the Old Covenant, priests were constantly on the go. While God had mercifully instituted a sacrificial system whereby atonement (covering) for sin could be made, the entire program was only temporary, ultimately pointing people to their need for God's permanent solution in the coming Messiah.

After Christ died and rose from the dead, He "sat down" at God's right hand, in part to send a very clear message to the Hebrews. That message was a banner of truth that we would be wise to continually keep before us today, for we are just as prone to legalism as the ancient Hebrews were. The message is simple: *The work is over!* Another way to say this was articulated by Jesus Himself on the cross, when He bellowed, "It is finished".[32]

The Levitical Priesthood instituted by God under the Old Covenant was an endless and bloody routine of constant sacrifice. There were no seats included in the temple furnishings for the priests to relax. Rotating in shifts, the priest would constantly receive sacrifices from the people – bringing them to the altar before God.

On the Day of Atonement, the high priest would sacrifice an unblemished lamb or goat on behalf of the collective sins of the nation. These sacrifices happened nonstop for many centuries under the old system. There was never a moment for the priest to sit down. Not so with Jesus.

As the High Priest of the New Covenant, Jesus' supremacy is the main event throughout the Book of Hebrews. Comparing Christ to the ordinary human priesthood, the author writes that "the ministry Jesus has received is as superior to theirs as the covenant of which he is mediator is superior to the old one, and it is *founded on better promises.*"[33]

What are those better promises? Hebrews 10:26 gives us the answer that in essence, "no sacrifice for sins is *needed* or *available* through anyone outside of the once-for-all sacrifice of Jesus. The work is complete. Count on it and choose to *rest* with Him!"

When we understand this context, we can enter into a chapter like Hebrews 10 without fear or confusion. The message is clear. In Hebrews 10:26, the "sin" being addressed is not in reference to the general sins we may commit, but to the *specific sin* of refusing to trust in and rely solely upon the "better promises" of the once-for-all sacrifice of Jesus.

Many Hebrew Christians, having come out of a life-long religious system of sacrificing at the temple, were understandably slow to break their habit of relying on the old way. Many were attempting to mix elements of new and old together, and this is the issue being addressed here.

The author of Hebrews is essentially saying, "Look, if we deliberately keep on sinning (by refusing to trust exclusively in Christ's finished work), we must remember that no sacrifice for sins (outside of Jesus Christ) is left!" In other words, *"There is no other valid source of forgiveness!* There is no other sacrificial offering that God will honor, because His Son has completed the rescue mission and *is presently sitting down*! The work is *over*! You are *wasting your time* by continuing to participate in the temple rituals because they are now obsolete and meaningless!"

Jesus-Plus: What is Really at Stake Here?

As stated previously, some teachers use this passage to insinuate that a believer can lose his or her salvation by deliberately persisting in sin. Others say that persisting in sin shows that the person was never truly saved at all. In reality, this passage teaches neither! Notice what the author does *not* say! He does *not* say that if these new Jewish followers of Jesus keep "sinning" by going to the temple that they will lose their salvation.

What he *does* say is that by failing to trust in the all-sufficient, once-for-all sacrifice of Jesus the High Priest, they were hurling themselves into a state of neurotic insecurity – a situation where no viable alternative remained!

By accepting a "Jesus-plus" mentality (in this case, Jesus-plus temple sacrifice) they were opening themselves up to the irrational yet horrific fear that they too might experience the same kind of judgment that awaits God's enemies. They were reverting to the no-win human system of never quite knowing for certain where they stood with God.

This insecurity was precisely what was fueling the "fearful expectation" of judgment mentioned in the passage. While the fear was irrational, it was nevertheless a natural outgrowth of failing to live by grace alone, pulling them away from the security and assurance that God desired for them to experience with Him.

The author's bold confrontation of this "Jesus-plus" mentality is all about seeking to build *assurance* into the lives of these early Hebrew Christians. The author didn't want them to remain insecure in their relationship with God!

Interestingly, proponents of both front-loading and back-loading the gospel will often accuse people like me of preaching what they call "gospel-lite" – a combative (and admittedly humorous) insinuation of watering the gospel down by being "overly" focused on the unconditional nature of grace apart from any demands outside of simple trust in Christ's finished work.

Even if those like myself were indeed guilty of this promoting "gospel-lite", what seems far more egregious in my opinion is the promulgation of what I would call "gospel-plus" theology. Whether it is *gospel-plus-requisites* or *gospel-plus-results* or *gospel-plus-baptism* or *gospel-plus-temple sacrifice* or *gospel-plus-whatever*, it is still the same issue being confronted by the author of Hebrews! Namely, that "gospel-plus" is no gospel at all and will leave even the genuine believer in a neurotic state of insecurity and legalistic bondage under the "fearful expectation of God's judgment". These are some of the very fears Jesus came to liberate us from!

No Other Gospel

Paul was so passionate about keeping the gospel *uncut* and *free* of human editorializing that he even got a little testy in his passionate defense of its purity. In Galatians, he issues an unusually caustic remark toward anyone who would alter the gospel of the free grace of Jesus Christ: *"Let (that person) be eternally condemned!"*[34]

Harsh verbiage from the Apostle of grace, yet these sentiments confirm the passion I too expressed in the opening pages of this book – that the Gospel is worth getting animated about! It is worth defending! For Paul it was even worth using shocking language as a means to wake people up to the reality of its utmost importance.

As someone who spent the bulk of his early spiritual journey paralyzed by fear, shame and the joy-robbing effects of religious duty – and now as a pastor who ministers to many people who struggle with similar debilitating habits – it has become my life's joy and passion to be a voice of liberation among those who have lost sight of the Jesus they originally fell in love with.

In the next section of this book, my hope is to speak with that voice. Having *unloaded* some of the major issues at hand, let us now walk together as we *unlearn* some of the false ideas many of us have embraced or assumed for so long. Let's take God's reputation out of the hands of angry sinners and listen carefully to what He says about Himself…

PART TWO: (UN)LEARN -
Letting Go of the Lies We've Believed

Chapter 5: Ruffling Feathers with the Grace of God

I have a little secret to confess. On occasion I enjoy using social media to post things that I'm confident will get a rise out of people. Don't judge me. You *know* you've done it too! Most of the time it's something funny or controversial (or both), with the intent to get people to think.

It seems automatic that whenever I post a comment about the lavish nature of God's grace, I get a mixture of both high enthusiasm and intense push-back. For the most part, I think people love to be reminded about the freely bestowed, unconditionally secure and flamboyantly generous divine welfare program that God has made available for the taking.

Yet when I post something about grace, there is inevitably someone who chimes in almost appearing as though it is their sacred duty to remind us that we'd better be careful not to neglect "the other side of the coin". In other words, *"Don't forget that our behavior matters to God!"*

Religious people from across the denominational spectrum can get downright uneasy when in their opinion grace is lifted "too high". I wonder why the mere mention of the utterly gratuitous nature of

God's grace is often so readily met by the well-meaning voices of those who immediately want to "balance" the discussion with talk about submitting Christ's Lordship or to point us to Paul's words in Romans 6 about not abusing grace as a license to sin?

Can we not for one moment simply pause to enjoy the final words of Romans 5, where Paul assures us that *"Where sin abounded, grace abounded all the more"*?[35] Granted, he strongly warned his audience against viewing grace as a license to sin, and he did so by explaining that we have died to sin and that sin is hurtful to ourselves and to the others it affects.

But let's be honest. When was the last time you felt like you needed a license to sin? Chances are, you became very good at sinning without even requiring a learner's permit! I know I did. Never once did my mother have to teach me *not* to share my possessions. Never once did I struggle to conjure up enough strength to yank a toy out of a playmate's hands and scream at the top of my lungs, *"Mine!"* Fact is, I was born with a doctorate degree in sinning and I've never needed a license to practice this kind of medicine!

To be sure, sin is contrary to the fellowship of God's Kingdom and to the fruit of His Spirit. We get it! Sin, bad. Obedience, good. At the same time, we *must* not forget that Paul's caution in the sixth chapter of Romans in no way negates or diminishes what he had previously established in Romans 5. If Christianity is the least bit unique from the claims of other faiths, this uniqueness rises and falls on the gratuitous and unconditional nature of grace!

> If Christianity is the least bit unique from the claims of other faiths, this uniqueness rises and falls on the gratuitous and unconditional nature of grace!

Either the gospel was and is a no-strings-attached offer of pardon, life and liberty that is free for the taking through faith alone – or it is an intrinsically evil bait-and-switch religious scheme promising a form of unconditional favor that it cannot actually deliver. I don't know about you, but sometimes my legalistic conscience alone can stir up enough self-condemnation to accuse a small village! As a Christian, I don't need to be constantly reminded *not* to use God's grace as a license to sin. That's fairly obvious!

Instead, I need to be reminded to rest upon an irrevocable expression of God's kindness that is so freely offered in Christ I have no other reasonable response than to lose myself in the awe of its reality! Then and only then will I escape the performance treadmill to which my inner Pharisee (also known as the *flesh*) longs to enslave me, and instead allow Jesus to live His supernatural life through me.

The popular *"try hard, fail, feel guilty, confess-your-sin-and-try-again"* routine is not the gospel Jesus or the Apostles came to proclaim. Yet those concepts vividly describe the spiritual experience of too many Christians. It is not uncommon for legalists and moralists to persistently remind us that Jesus commanded His followers to come and *die* in order to find life, as if these words were central to the New Covenant message of the gospel.

But as we have already noted in the first section of this book, these voices either ignore or significantly downplay the fact that Jesus' words were stated in a specific theological and historic context. His words – precious as they are – must not be stripped from this context and given new meaning under the guise that "Jesus said it, so you'd better accept it." That's a dangerous way to interpret the Bible.

Christ's commands to come and die, deny oneself, take up our cross, etc. were given while still living under the realities of the Old System, the Old Covenant way of life. As we discussed in chapter 2 related to the Sermon on the Mount, much of Jesus' intention in His public teaching was to set the stage for receiving the New System He was about to inaugurate. We cannot forget that Jesus was "born under law, to redeem those under law…" (Galatians 4:4-5).

Ministering under the auspices of the Old Covenant, Jesus would often set the bar *so* high that nobody could even *pretend* to have reached it. He did this on purpose to get the nation of Israel to admit Her utter helplessness before a holy God in order that She might freely receive the New in place of the Old! Everything Jesus spoke about prior to His death on the cross was expressed under the Old System, setting Israel (and ultimately every one of us) up to admit our failure so we could receive the New System with joy and gratitude.

Of course, this reality does not negate the possibility that a believer may experience persecution for their faith. In that sense, a "taking up of one's cross" may apply as it did with Christ's eleven disciples, all of whom except John died a martyr's death. However, the kind of "taking up the cross" we see in the lives of persecuted believers does not insinuate that a rigorous attitude of self-denial is either a prerequisite for salvation *or* a formula for Christian living!

A "Come and Die" Gospel?

After the cross and resurrection, the Apostles no longer preached that disciples of Jesus must "die" in order to follow Him. Never do you hear this kind of language from Paul, Peter, John or James. Instead, they proclaimed a radically different message – that believers are to "reckon" themselves dead to sin and alive to God in Christ – past tense, permanent reality. To reckon means to "consider it true by faith" (see Romans 6:11).

This is much more than a minor technicality or matter of mere semantics. This is a vital difference in the way we are to view salvation and discipleship. *Before* the cross, the disciples were challenged to follow Jesus by dying to themselves. Of course, this was at best a series of inconsistent ups and downs in the real world. *After* the cross and resurrection, believers were to reckon themselves *dead already* by faith in their spiritual identification with Christ's finished work (Romans 6:11; Galatians 2:20) and then to *live by faith* from that new, righteous identity.

New Covenant discipleship is not a matter of laying down one's life in order to "be like the Master". Instead it is to reckon oneself dead *already* so that the Master lives *through the disciple* as the very Life within that person. That this opportunity is both possible and preferable for the Christian is the greatest practical effect of the uncut gospel upon our daily lifestyle.

As we have already established, mandating that this victorious life in Christ be a litmus test for whether a person can truly rest assured of their salvation goes *way* beyond what Scripture intends to tell us. Simply put, if grace were not open to the possibility of abuse, it would at that very moment cease to be grace!

As I explained in chapter 3 when discussing the false claims of some advertisers, if I gave you a gift and then told you that in order for you to know for sure you get to keep it you must serve me as your master, the gift would then cease to be a gift. I may have freely offered it on the front end of the deal, but I would have back-loaded the gift with the mandatory "results" that I wanted to see. That is precisely how many Evangelicals relate to the gospel. They view God's grace as a bilateral *transaction* rather than a unilateral *action* whereby God gives us a free gift expecting nothing in return in terms of either earning or proving that it is really ours.

> ... if grace were not open to the possibility of abuse, it would at that very moment cease to be grace!

But What About Good Works?

As a teenager, I remember having the question asked of me by an over-zealous youth leader, *"If you were accused of being a Christian in a court of law, would there be enough evidence to send you to prison?"* The point of the question was obviously to encourage me to examine whether I was truly "living what I claimed to believe."

The very idea of God's gift of grace being a no-strings-attached offer is appalling to those who misunderstand the uncut gospel. As an outgrowth of *Perseverance of the Saints*, LS assumes that all truly saved people will in *every case* begin to walk in gradual (if not immediate) victory over sin in this life. While every Christian leader I know would certainly *want* this to be the case, to demand that it *must* be is to stretch the Bible beyond what it teaches about the faith-and-works relationship.

LS theology over-emphasizes performance as a "litmus test" for one's assurance of salvation. In truth, the only Biblical "litmus test" is whether or not a person trusts in the simple promise of Christ to save those who simply *believe* in the work of His cross and empty tomb. As we have seen, passages like James 2 and Hebrews 10 are commonly used to promote this litmus-test mentality.

LS advocates routinely accuse believers in the uncut gospel of encouraging people to think they are saved even if there appears to be little or no "proof" to back it up. They claim that telling people the truth about the meaning of repentance will lead to a non-chalant mental affirmation about the facts of the gospel without any real heart-level change.

But as we have established, the word *repenentance* means "a change of mind" in the sense of changing one's *perspective*. No one I am aware of who endorses the uncut gospel of grace is claiming that anyone is truly a Christian if they can bring themselves to believe that the crucifixion happened as a mere fact of history. Faith in the uncut gospel is believing that Jesus did these things for us *personally* and that His finished work alone saves us. It is a *change of perspective*, not just mental assent to an impersonal historic event.

Believers and Burgers

To put it another way, let's say I am driving down the road planning to stop at my favorite burger joint for a cheeseburger and fries. On the way I see a sign in the window of a delicatesson that says: *Footlong Turkey Sandwich – Five Dollars.*

If at that moment the advertisement convinces me that the five dollar sandwich is a better deal and I choose to eat at the deli over the burger joint as a result, I have merely changed my mind based on random factual information. This doesn't necessarily mean however, that I've changed my perspective. It just means I'm looking for a good deal.

Now let's carry that analogy one step further. Suppose I am addicted to cheeseburgers. In fact, tonight I am planning on having a burger and fries for dinner as I do almost every night. It has become my routine to spend countless hours in the evening perusing photos of the juiciest burgers on the internet before deciding which greasy "house of sin" I will visit that night.

As I am surfing the pictures and advertisements, I stumble across an online nutrition facts chart comparing cheeseburgers with turkey sandwiches. As I read through the facts, I realize that there is no real nutritional comparison. The deli sandwich is a far healthier choice and I begin to understand that by eating nutritious food instead of habitually raiding the burger joint, I will probably extend the duration and quality of my life.

It is at this point that I have experienced more than a random change of mind. I have truly changed my perspective. I have *repented*, having been convinced of the truth on a personal level. Why would I want to fill my body with my old choice of food when I can get something that is so much better for me?

At this point my perspective has been changed not because of some slick advertisement, but because I have truly encountered *reality* and have concluded that if I don't make the switch, my health and future could be at stake. This is essentially what happens when we go from unbelief to belief in Christ. We don't just believe he died *factually*. We believe that He died for us *personally*.

Contrary to what many within the LS camp suggest, defenders of the uncut gospel care deeply about this change of perspective leading to a change in lifestyle. Yet ironically, the consistent teaching of Jesus and the Apostles is focused on a much *greater* danger than the possibility of abusing grace as a license to sin.

In reality, the New Testament affirms that it is far more likely for a person to *mistakenly* believe they are saved by virtue of the fact that good works *are* present in their lives! This is classic self-righteousness and pure legalism in its rawest form.

This is why many pseudo-Christian cultic groups offer a false assurance of salvation to their adherents. They have the good works to make them feel like they're "proving it", while simultaneously believing a false gospel. The great irony of the gospel message of Jesus and the Apostles is that our only means of "qualification" is to admit our utter *disqualification* and instead trust Christ alone to be our life and righteousness.

If this trust is what is meant by "repentance" (i.e. changing one's mind from unbelief to belief in Christ's finished work), then this kind of repentance is an aspect of genuine faith in Christ. If on the other hand, repentance is defined as "turning from sin" and is viewed as a mandatory *requisite for* or *result of* justification, this is a false understanding of the gospel according to the teaching of the New Testament.

When I teach about the reality of Jesus' teachings being directed to those under the Law, it is not uncommon for people to ask for a Scriptural example of Him pointing people to the gospel of grace. We might naturally wonder whether Jesus said *anything* that pertains to the New Covenant way of life.

The answer of course, is *yes He did*! Jesus constantly pointed His audience forward to the coming hope of the saving work He would soon accomplish! These examples are numerous, and in the next chapter we will discuss one of the most prolific – the famous story of the Lost Son. But first, a bit more about our assurance and security in Christ.

Assurance: Does it Really Matter?

Among the many who espouse LS, there is a general tendency to downplay the importance of our need for assurance of salvation. While I cannot pretend to speak for every one of them, this downplaying is often founded on the bizarre notion that a certain amount of insecurity may actually be *beneficial* in a believer's life, at least for keeping the rebellious behaviors of some people in check.

By contrast, most who believe in the uncut gospel would affirm that assurance of salvation is not only possible, but *essential* for healthy spiritual growth to occur in our lives! So why this descrepency in passion over this issue? And more importantly, what does the New Testament really teach about assurance?

First, I want to consider the question: *What is assurance of salvation and why does it matter?* Essentially, the *security of our salvation* is based upon God's numerous *objective* promises never to disown His children or divorce His bride, depending on which metaphor you prefer.

In contrast, our *assurance of salvation* is related to the *subjective* peace and confidence we experience in knowing that we are irreversibly loved, forgiven and saved by God. While our eternal security in Christ can never change because it is an objective truth, our assurance of salvation *can* come under attack based on what we believe about God and His gospel

Assurance of salvation is immensely important. While some would suggest that a certain amount of insecurity is good in motivating us to "examine ourselves", the fact is that entertaining such doubt is futile according to Scripture and plain reason. For one thing, no human behaves perfectly *or* has the ability to judge with flawless objectivity. Not to acknowledge this can lead us into those fear-producing, unanswerable questions like *Am I committed enough? Am I bearing enough fruit? What if I fail to break out of this sinful pattern? Am I surrendered enough to Christ as master over my life?*

Most people use one solitary verse to argue for the alleged need to "examine ourselves". It is found in 2 Corinthians 13:5, where Paul says, "Examine yourselves as to whether you are in the faith. Test yourselves. Do you not know yourselves, that Jesus Christ is in you? – unless indeed you are disqualified."

Almost every time I speak to someone who minimizes the importance of assurance, this is the verse they will mention to support their view that we shouldn't be over-confident. But if I *must* say it again, paying attention to the context of this verse means *everything* in helping us see that Paul is not suggesting Christians should doubt their salvation.

What is actually happening here is that Paul has spent huge portions of the previous chapters defending the genuineness of his authority as true apostle against the claims of false apostles who were trying to question the legitimacy of his leadership in the early Church. In response, Paul is saying "Why are you bringing *my* legitimacy into question? Why are you casting doubt upon *my* ministry? Examine your *own* qualifications to see whether *you* are truly one of us!"

This is not a passage about individual believers practicing some so-called "discipline of examination" to determine whether they are truly "in the faith." In context, it is a rebuke to false apostles who were creeping into legitimate Christian circles with messages that were contradictory or counter-productive to the gospel of grace, in addition to undermining Paul's apostolic authority.

Assurance Matters, and Here's Why...

If you are well-acquainted with Evangelical Christianity, you have undoubtedly heard the name John Piper. While I have never personally met him, I have read many of his books and perceive him to be someone who loves Jesus deeply. For that I respect him.

While John Piper's passion for global missions, his emphasis on God's glory and his pastoral concern for personal holiness in the church are highly commendable, the following examples raise concern among many of those who believe that assurance of salvation is critical to a healthy and fruitful Christian life. I mention Dr. Piper by name only because of his vast influence and my belief that his views are representative of many who share in his LS perspective.

In a lecture given in 2007, Piper offered some words which deeply surprised many Evangelical believers. Responding to a question about the possibility of having assurance of salvation, he offered the honest admission: "...why I sin against my wife the same at age sixty-two that I did at age forty-two causes me sometimes to doubt my salvation."[36] Now read that sentence again.

Do you see anything concerning about this statement? This high-profile, greatly-admired Christian leader sometimes doubts his salvation based upon the way he occasionally treats his wife? One of the leading voices among Evangelical Christian leaders wrestles with moments of doubt about his very salvation because of long-standing imperfections in his life?

What kind of theology produces this? Some might say that this was simply either a use of hyberbole or a humble admission of his own human frailty. But we would be wise to consider whether it could be the result of a deeper problem.

I find it interesting that both hyper-Calvinism *and* extreme Arminianism can have a similar affect among followers of either system: *spiritual insecurity*. For the hyper-Calvinist, the litmus-test mindset can invoke a preoccupation with heavy introspection, producing a neurotic, ongoing subliminal search for enough "evidence" to *feel* saved and legitimate as a believer.

For the Arminian, there is the incessant fear that given enough unconfessed sin or moral failure, he or she could be in danger of losing their salvation, and therefore in need of being "born again... again" through some heartfelt re-affirmation of faith coupled with a rededicated promise of obedience. But are either of these among God's intentions for a Biblical Christian life?

Piper goes on to admit that among his followers he encounters a considerable level of insecurity related to the issue of assurance:

> I deal with this as much as anything, probably, in the people that I'm preaching to. Fears – and doubts – doubts not about objective 'Did He rise from the dead'...very few people are wrestling with that. But 'Am I in? Am I saved?' That's *very common for people to wrestle with.*[37]

Very common for people to wrestle with? That may be true in Piper's circles, but why? Is assurance of salvation possible? Is it Biblical? Is it *essential* or even the least bit *important* to the Christian experience? The pages of the New Testament undeniably answer this question in the affirmative!

In fact, based upon the sheer volume and clarity of passages related to assurance, it is bewildering that some could so easily downplay or even miss this issue entirely! Consider the following small sampling:

> I write these things to you who believe in the name of the Son of God *so that you may know that you have eternal life.* (1 John 5:13)

> ...being confident of this, that *he who began a good work in your will carry it on to completion* until the day of Christ Jesus. (Philippians 1:6)

Praise be to the God and Father of our Lord Jesus Christ! In his great mercy he has given us new birth into a living hope through the resurrection of Jesus Christ from the dead, and into *an inheritance that can never perish, spoil or fade—kept in heaven for you*, who through faith are *shielded by God's power until the coming of the salvation* that is ready to be revealed in the last time. (1 Peter 1:3-5)

Therefore, if anyone is in Christ, *he is a new creation*; the old has gone, the new has come! (2 Corinthians 5:17)

...*if we are faithless, he will remain faithful*, for he cannot disown himself. (2 Timothy 2:13)

And you also were included in Christ when you heard the word of truth, the gospel of your salvation. Having believed, *you were marked in him with a seal*, the promised Holy Spirit, who is a deposit *guaranteeing our inheritance until the redemption of those who are God's possession*—to the praise of his glory. (Ephesians 1:13-14)

For I am convinced that neither death nor life, neither angels nor demons, neither the present nor the future, nor any powers, neither height nor depth, *nor anything else in all creation, will be able to separate us from the love of God that is in Christ Jesus our Lord*. (Romans 8:38-39)

Security and Maturity – Which Comes First?

At the local church where I serve as a pastor, I frequently remind God's people of the New Covenant reality that *our security is the basis for our maturity* – not vice versa. In this book I have been making the case that if the gospel is a bait-and-switch offer of a disingenuous "free gift" on the front side with any works-based conditions whatsoever on the flip side, then it is *not* the uncut gospel of the New Covenant. Those who believe Romans 2:4 – that it is God's *kindness* that leads people to a change of mind and heart – cannot promote introspection-based assurance when the Scriptures allow for no such thing!

Assurance of salvation is not a "peripheral issue" in the realm of practical Christian living. It is foundational – not only to the daily Christian lifestyle, but also to the preaching of the gospel itself. It bears repeating that the moment we begin to rely upon our performance rather than solely upon the unconditional promises of Christ ("believe in Me and be saved") is the moment we lose sight of the gospel of grace and begin sinking into the quicksand of legalism.

> Assurance of salvation is not a "peripheral issue" in the realm of practical Christian living. It is foundational – not only to the daily Christian lifestyle, but also to the preaching of the gospel itself.

In the next chapter, we will discover the unconditional nature of God's grace toward His children through one of Christ's most famous stories designed to point people to the Gospel Uncut...

Chapter 6: The Gospel Jesus Revealed

O f all of the stories, parables and teachings of Jesus, there is one in which the heart of the uncut gospel shines through like a beacon on a dark, foggy night. It definitely stands out as one of the many "clear" passages of Scripture by which our understanding of the handful of allegedly "cloudy" texts must be illuminated.

In Luke 15:11-32 Jesus gives to Israel, and to every human being on the planet, a summary of his or her own life story. While each precise detail may not literally describe the actions of every single person, the point becomes rather obvious that the message of the story is for anyone willing to see themselves in the characters Jesus presents.

The Lost Son

As you may be aware, the drama focuses on a rebellious lad who abruptly asks his dad for his inheritance prematurely only to squander the wealth on drunken escapades, wild sex and other forms of intense hedonistic escapism. What is so awe-inspiring is that Jesus is telling this story knowing full well that there are many in the crowd who are angry about His own seemingly *irresponsible* grace toward everyday "sinners." Luke explains

Now the tax collectors and "sinners" were all gathering around to hear him. But the Pharisees and the teachers of the law muttered, "This man welcomes sinners and eats with them."[38]

The story of the rebellious son highlights some astonishing realities that we can apply to our lives whenever we need reassurance concerning the overtly gratuitous nature of the gospel. For anyone whose past is checkered with things they are ashamed of, or whose current addictions and life-dominating sins have them constantly looking over their shoulder, the story trumpets a startling and scandalous perspective of God's grace.

Grace Always Allows for Freedom to Make Choices

For starters, it is because of the nature of God's *love* that He offers us freedom to make choices. Any view of love that is not based upon freedom of choice signifies a gross misunderstanding of the Biblical concept. God could have chosen to keep humanity on a short, robotic leash, but He did not.

From the beginning, Adam and Eve were given the capacity to exercise their volition – their will. This is a core belief within Biblical Christianity – that God, without conceding one shred of His sovereignty, allows humans to make genuine choices of the will. Of course, there are often earthly consequences resulting from disobedience, and such was the case with the rebellious son in Jesus' parable.

The passage tells us that this young man wasted his entire inheritance living on the wild side. Later in the story we find out that much of it went to sexual encounters with prostitutes. And after he'd partied it all away....he was left with the haunting reality that he had ruined everything.

Can you envision the guilt and shame he must have felt over the situation he'd created? Jesus' mention in verse 16 of the fact that he wished he could eat the pig food was an indication of just how low he felt. Pigs were considered the most detestable, unclean animal in Jewish culture. Christ's point would have fallen on the ears of his audience with penetrating clarity: this man was detestable and unclean in his own eyes, and would have also been viewed this way by everyone else.

It is telling that Jesus didn't try to argue with the Pharisees about the fact that He spent an inordinate amount of time hanging out with society's failures and misfits. By sharing this story, Jesus agrees with the Pharisees that the "sinners" he was loving *had* in fact walked in abject rebellion against the commands of God. In many cases, they *deserved* the very messes they had created. Moreover, they deserved judgment rather than mercy and Jesus never denies that point.

But suddenly, as if to purposefully deflect their condemnation – as if to totally undermine the ground upon which these Pharisees thought they were safely standing – Jesus shifts the focus of the story from the *failure* of the son to the *faithfulness* of the Father. The story continues…

> When he (the rebellious son) came to his senses, he said, "How many of my father's hired men have food to spare, and here I am starving to death! I will set out and go back to my father and say to him: Father, I have sinned against heaven and against you. I am *no longer worthy to be called your son;* make me like one of your hired men." So he got up and went to his father. But *while he was still a long way off, his father saw him and was filled with compassion for him; he ran to his son, threw his arms around him and kissed him.* The son said to him, "Father, I have sinned against heaven and against you. I am *no longer worthy* to be called your son." (Luke 15:17-21)

Here, Jesus introduces a radically different understanding of God through the character of the father in the story, which leads to a second major reality concerning grace…

Grace is Always Greater than our Failures

It had always been the case even throughout the Old Testament. The sacrificial system under Moses was proof of the fact that while sin was very serious to God, He was also serious about providing a *substitutionary* sacrifice for it so that His people could enjoy relationship with Him. That former system was a temporary structure under which God would overlook sin. As we explore Jesus' story in further detail, consider some of the specific failures that the Father overlooks, even as it is being told from an Old Covenant point of reference among the audience of Pharisees.

1) Grace is Greater than our Mixed Motives

With regard to this famous tale of redemption, I hear preachers focus primarily on the boy's supposed contrition, insinuating that the father was responding kindly mostly because of his son's genuine change of heart. I'm not so sure I believe that. To be certain, the boy was *regretful* for the predicament that he'd created for himself. But consider his words: "...how many of my father's hired men have food to spare, and here I am starving to death" (vs. 17).

Can you see it? The son is definitely bummed about the quandary he has gotten himself into. But if we deal honestly with the story Jesus is telling, it seems as though the young man is more concerned with the discomfort he's created for *himself* than about the heartache of his father!

Christian philosophers and psychologists agree that for a change of behavior to occur in a person struggling with a life-dominating sin or addiction, they must finally come out of denial. Often this includes arriving at the place where the pain of *remaining* in the sin outweighs the pain that may be required to change. Here's the point: While God *always* gives grace to the humble, the uncut gospel offers us grace *even* when our hearts are still very self-centered.

This was a huge relief for me to discover when I was stuck in the rut of ruthlessly and regularly beating myself up with routines of morbid introspection. I somehow felt that any motive to avoid sin outside of pure passion for God was less than admirable in His eyes. But in this tale, the Father seems to be saying, *"My child, when you are finally sick and tired of the chaos you've created, just come to me. When the pain is finally too much for you to bear and you have nowhere else to turn, just come to me. My arms are open, even if your motives are still mixed! Simply come and allow me to love you!"*

By this, Jesus was directly confronting a popular false-doctrine known to his audience as *Divine Retribution*. It was an idea held by many religious folks based on the notion that God will pay you back for your sin, because after all, that's what you deserve! This idea had become so rooted in the culture that the ancient Jewish communities would often practice a ritual called *Kezazeh*. Author Jeff Lucas does a great job explaining this phenomenon in his book *The Prodigal-Friendly Church*[39]. Allow me to briefly summarize.

Kezazeh was the Aramaic word that meant "cutting off". It was a devastating ritual similar to a funeral, although it was administered to someone who was not yet dead! It symbolized the total rejection and alienation of a person who had fallen into disfavor with a family or community. The ritual literally communicated, "You are nothing – banished – unwelcomed. You are forever divorced from the community. Pack your bags and get out of town!"

Kezazeh was enacted for many reasons, one of the most common of which was whenever a Jewish boy lost his inheritance among the Gentile population and attempted to return home. It was against this cultural backdrop that Jesus was telling this tale.

In such a case as this, the boy would likely be met by an angry mob shouting words of intimidation. The group would then proceed to break clay pots filled with pebbles as a ceremonial symbol of the irreversibly broken relationship with the community.

It was essentially their version of the Scarlet Letter! You were *done* – the only exception being that you could *prove* your remorse by working off your debt! This explains why the son in Jesus' story offers to work his way back into good standing with the father.

The point Jesus was making? As it turns out, God *doesn't* repay us according to what our sins deserve! The uncut gospel invites us to come to the Father *expecting* unconditional acceptance – a reality that sounds *much* too good to be true to Pharisees of both yesterday and today! And with this we discover another failure that grace enabled the father to overlook…

2) Grace is Greater than our Pretending

Not only is God's grace greater than our mixed motives, but it is greater than our false pretense as well. Once again, at first glance the son seems sincere. He offers the confession, "I have sinned against heaven and against you!" Many preachers point to this phrase to again argue that the father only took the son back because of his sincere "repentance". But is this *really* the point?

One curious fact is that the boy's confession was virtually identical to the words of Pharaoh when he was *faking* repentance to Moses as recorded in one of the most famous stories of the Torah! In Exodus 10, after God had used Moses to bring numerous plagues of judgment against the Egyptians, Pharaoh summoned Moses and Aaron saying, "I have sinned against the LORD your God and against you" (vs. 16). The confession sounded so sincere, but only a short time later Pharaoh was right back to his old ways, oppressing God's people and worshiping false idols.

The Pharisees knew the story of Pharaoh like the back of their hands. Could it be that Jesus was alluding to the familiar words of this passage to notify these legalists that God's grace is *so* astounding that is even willing to overlook our partial phoniness – our pretending – if we will but come back to Him? I believe so, and I raise the question to encourage us realize how highly the grace of God is being esteemed in this passage.

"I have sinned against heaven and against you…" Was this a sincere statement from the young man's heart? It was definitely well-rehearsed, and we may never know for sure. But it is worth pointing out that the Father, almost unbelievably, is willing to overlook even our phony posturing when we approach Him! He understands our brokenness and will even overlook our pretending! This brings us to a third failure overlooked by the father in the story…

3) Grace is Greater than our Self-righteousness

Consider carefully the phrase "I am no longer worthy to be called your son" (vs. 19). Those words sound so pious, don't they? But what exactly does the boy mean by the phrase *"no longer worthy"*?

When we read that phrase we are forced to wonder what on earth made him think that his *worthiness* was what qualified him to be the father's child in the first place! The young man was not a child of his father because he had earned that right. Rather, he was a child of his father for *one* simple reason: he was *born* to him!

How many times have we allowed deep feelings of unworthiness, though they may feel like humility, to keep us from resting securely in the gentle arms of the Father? I remember the day when this light bulb went on for me, as God used this story of the lost son to affirm that He has *never* accepted or loved me because of my worthiness. His opinion of me is not *caused* by anything I ever did or failed to do. He loves me simply because I belong to Him! Through faith, I have been spiritually "born" to Him, and this relationship is eternal and irreversible.

Self-righteousness can be such a deceptive posture! Disguising itself as humility, it can make us feel very spiritual as we lament the state of our unworthiness. And while in and of ourselves our unworthiness is a fact, it also underscores the entire *reason* for

> By definition, grace applies *only* to the unworthy!

grace in the first place! By definition, grace applies *only* to the unworthy! Only when we catch this reality are we ready to move on in utter gratitude to another reality. Not only does grace provide us with freedom to choose. Not only does grace overlook our failure. But thirdly...

Grace Always Extends Total Forgiveness and Restoration

In Luke 15:22-24 the story continues,

> But the father said to his servants, "Quick! Bring the best robe and put it on him. Put a ring on his finger and sandals on his feet. Bring the fattened calf and kill it. Let's have a feast and

celebrate. For this son of mine was dead and is alive again; he was lost and is found. So they began to celebrate."

The further into the story Jesus leads us, the clearer the message becomes. The Father of Jesus not only overlooks our failures, but actually provides full reconciliation so that fellowship can never be broken.

The Pharisees listening to the story would have considered it benevolence enough had the father merely allowed his son to work as his slave. This probably would have been on the mind of the son also. As I noted earlier, his only hope would have been the slim possibility that the father might have allowed him to work off his debt. Instead, we find scandalously gracious words flowing from the lips of the father: "Bring the best robe and put it on him.....for....he was lost and is found."

This business about a robe and a ring and a fattened calf was all the stuff associated with a full-fledged family reunion! You might notice that the father seems almost irresponsibly dismissive in the way that he fails to even entertain the son's confession. He is simply overwhelmed with gladness to be holding his son in a warm embrace!

Admittedly, the father's disposition sounds *much* too good to be true! This is a story of scandalous grace! It is a story that infuriated the Pharisees of the first century as much as it infuriates the legalists of today! Grace is not fair. Grace doesn't seem to hold the offender accountable. In short, grace uses very fuzzy math. And that brings us to a fourth and final reality we need to catch from the story...

Grace Frustrates the Self-righteous

The tale continues by shedding light on the character of the older brother. This is where we discover that the story is really *more* than just about a lost son – but rather, lost *sons*. The first son is lost in the sin of *license* while the second is lost in the sin of *legalism*. Jesus goes on to say in Luke 15:25-29,

> Meanwhile, the older son....answered his father, "Look! All these years I've been slaving for you and never disobeyed your

orders. Yet you never even gave me a young goat so I could celebrate with my friends."

This exchange reveals a sobering reality: grace is a blatant offense to the Pharisee in each of us. It doesn't feel right when we see it applied in certain circumstances. It doesn't seem fair, and the reaction of the older brother highlights this glaring truth. And while it is certainly *not* fair that an innocent victim (Jesus) had to die in our place because of our sin, that fact is nonetheless the central reality of the uncut gospel.

The Bible repeatedly affirms that because God is just, He must punish sin. Any God who would simply overlook the injustice of the world without ultimate punishment would be *neither* a God of love *or* justice. And that's where the genius of the cross enters into the picture! The cross is the place where the *grace* and *wrath* of God collide.

The essence of the uncut gospel is simply this: The Father sent Jesus to suffer the punishment that *we* deserved so that we could in essence, get off scot-free! Once we become the recipients of that *free* gift through belief in Jesus alone, there is nothing we can do to either erase *or* enhance our standing before God.

This is where true assurance of salvation is rooted. Even when the prodigal son was living in total rebellion, he never for one moment ceased to be his father's child. This story illustrates a reality for two basic types of people.

The *first* type is the person who has never trusted in Christ in order to become a child of God. If you, for example, have never trusted in Jesus' payment for your sin on the cross, the Bible says that you stand condemned because you are rejecting God's free payment for your sin.[40] The answer to your dilemma is very simple: you are invited to place faith in Jesus and find complete and eternal forgiveness – no fine print attached!

The *second* type includes those who *have* become children of God through belief in Jesus, but have struggled to enjoy the intimacy that is ever available with God because of a persistent lifestyle that brings pain to the heart of the father and shame to oneself. This person is the kind who is stuck in some form of addiction or life-dominating sin and for whatever reason, has not been willing and/or able to walk by the Spirit's power in becoming free from it.

There are many reasons people contrive in order to avoid enjoying intimacy with God. Some people love their sin and are at a point where they have been fooled into believing that sin can be "managed". These folks may pay destructive earthly consequences for their behavior, but as children of God they can never be severed from the Father's eternal grace, love and restoring power.

Others are people who live like I did for so long, resisting intimacy with God because of a prideful sense of unworthiness that "feels" like humility, but is really nothing more than a lame excuse for not allowing Jesus to love them the way He desires to!

I don't know what your issue is. But if you hear nothing else from this chapter, hear this: *It is time to come to the Father*! His grace is powerful and permanent, and can never be lost once gained through trusting in Christ's sacrifice as your only means of relationship with God. When Christ cried from the cross "It is finished," He meant it. There is nothing you can do to improve or diminish God's opinion of you as His child. No huffing and puffing to impress or appease God is necessary. Brennan Manning says it so well:

> When Christ cried from the cross "It is finished," He meant it. There is nothing you can do to improve or diminish God's opinion of you as His child.

> God is not moody or capricious; He knows no seasons of change. He has a single relentless stance toward us: He loves us. He is the only God who loves sinners. False gods – the gods of human manufacturing – despise sinners, but the Father of Jesus loves all, no matter what they do. But of course this is almost too incredible for us to accept. Nevertheless, the central affirmation of the Reformation stands: through no merit of ours, but by His mercy, we have been restored

to a right relationship with God through the life, death, and resurrection of His beloved Son. This is the Good News, the gospel of grace.[41]

The Older Brother

Again, we typically think of Jesus' story in Luke 15 as the story of the rebellious son when in reality we should think of it in terms of rebellious *sons*. Seeing the characters as metaphorical for the present day, there are many people I have met who resist coming to the Father *not* because they are unattracted to Jesus, but because they are intimidated by the "older brother," so to speak.

In other words, they would never darken the doors of a church because they are fearful of the judgmental rejection they might expect from those in the church whom they perceive to be self-righteous and critical. This is not only true in America, but also in every foreign missions context in which I have traveled. It is high time the Body of Christ began to lay down the idolatry of self-righteousness – often disguised as personal "holiness" – and begin welcoming with open arms those who Jesus came to seek and save.

Finally, of the many powerful messages we discover from this story, one of the most compelling is also the least complicated: we cannot fix ourselves. Self-righteousness is essentially just that – an attitude that suggests we can somehow "make something up" to God for the strikes we have against us. This independent, self-sufficient attitude is essentially the root of all sin.

When Adam and Eve first sinned in the Garden of Eden, the narrative in no way suggests that Eve was intentionally shaking her fist in God's face as rebellion against Him. Her fall was a more subtle, seemingly naïve occurrence. It was a failure to depend upon God's Word and His provision. She listened to the enemy of her soul telling her that trusting God was not essential, and that she should do things her own way. And of course, Adam followed suit.

After this initial sin of seeking independence from God, we see its tragic consequences begin to snowball as Adam and Eve attempt to atone for (cover up) their own mistake by their own means. In chapter

1 we noted that in a pathetic and quite literal attempt to conceal their shame, they "sewed fig leaves together and made coverings for themselves" (Genesis 3:7).

What is so wonderful is that in the midst of this tragedy, we see God make the first blood sacrifice recorded in the Bible and cover them with the animal skin, foreshadowing a sacrificial system that would ultimately find it's fulfillment in the superior, once-for-all blood sacrifice of Jesus Christ. Jesus' sacrifice did not merely *cover* sin, but entirely *removed* it from our record as well as from our core nature, eradicating our guilt. This was something that the blood of mere animals could never do, according to Hebrews 10:3-4.[42]

Later on we will further discuss God's removal of our sin nature through the New Covenant, but with all this talk about God's amazing grace, it is important for us to scratch an itch that all this grace-talk seems to generate – the answer to the question: *Who really cares about sin?*

Chapter 7: Who Really Cares About Sin?

A s I have tried to explain, one of the cries of resistance I hear most often from both legalists *and* well-meaning Christians when I proclaim the message of the uncut gospel is this: *"What about sin? If people actually believe that they are forgiven no matter what – won't they just abuse that message as a license to sin all the more?"*

Evidently, the Apostle Paul dealt with these types of questions related to the gospel he lived and taught. After Paul spent the first 5 chapters of Romans offering painstaking detail in defense of the free grace of God against all forms of self-righteousness, he concludes chapter 5 with the precious words, "But where sin increased, grace increased all the more…" (vs. 20).

Then and only then – either anticipating or answering the questions of his critics – does Paul raise the question, *"What shall we say then? Shall we go on sinning so that grace may increase?"* And his answer was clear: *"By no means! We died to sin; how can we live in it any longer?"* (Romans 6:1-2).

Paul dealt with this concern very openly in Romans, and he makes it clear that the Spirit of God desires to change the behavior of believers over the course of their spiritual journey with Him. With regard to these issues there are some definite points that need to be made at the onset.

First, to say that Christians are *"forgiven no matter what"* is not the same as saying *"God doesn't care about sin."* To insinuate that advocates of the uncut gospel teach this would almost be hilarious if it were not so untrue. The so-called "cheap grace" that some legalists enjoy accusing people like me of promoting is in reality *anything but* cheap. Grace is *free* to the recipient, but certainly not cheap! In fact, grace required the blood of God's Son to be shed on the cross in the place of every sinner who actually *did* deserve the death penalty.

Obviously, God cares deeply about sin and so should we. He cares so much about it that He took the most drastic, sacrificial measures in order to deal permanently with its consequences. And yet the cross proves that the only thing eclipsing God's holy hatred of sin is His furious love for sinners.

> ... the cross proves that the only thing eclipsing God's holy hatred of sin is His furious love for sinners.

God hates sin not because He is a cranky old man upstairs trying to spoil our fun. He hates sin for greater reasons, including its affects on those He loves so much! He hates sin because its root came from an attitude of choosing independence from Him beginning with Satan and then with Adam and Eve. He knows that independence from Him is a clear and consistent path toward disaster.

At the cross, God enacted the perfect scenario through which He could adequately judge sin by placing it's punishment upon a *Representative of* and *Substitute for* the human race while granting sinners total pardon at Christ's expense. To distort this message in any way, shape or form is to infringe upon the purity of the uncut gospel of Jesus Christ.

A second point that must be reiterated is that Paul's statement in Romans 6:1-2 about not living in sin any longer, while true, in no way negates or minimizes his previous affirmation regarding the bottomless tank of God's grace offered to through Jesus. In other words, the fact that we are no longer held hostage by the power of sin in no way undermines the previous reality that "where sin increased, grace increased all the more" (Romans 5:20).

The truth is that life-transformation is *never* the by-product of spiritual insecurity. Living under a persistent sense of God's disapproval – or in some cases blatant fear of His wrath – never has and never will transform a single life. Manipulation through fear may temporarily *reform* a pattern of behavior, but it will never help a person truly grow in demonstration of the character of Jesus.

Early in his letter to the Romans, Paul established the fact that it is God's "kindness" that leads a person to repentance, not fear of His wrath or striving to earn His approval.[43] The uncut gospel is a proclamation of the reality that God is not angry with His children!

> The uncut gospel is a proclamation of the reality that God is not angry with His children!

One hundred percent of God's righteous anger against sin has been satisfied at the cross! We noted already that this is a non-negotiable Christian belief called "propitiation." Jesus Christ absorbed the wrath of God when He became sin for us, "so that in him we might become the righteousness of God" (2 Corinthians 5:21).

Motivation vs. Manipulation

Yes, sin is serious to God. And no, He does not want for it to dominate your life. Yet the reality is that if fear of God's displeasure is fueling your journey, you will never experience the transforming work of the Spirit's power! Grace motivates, but fear manipulates! A bait-and-switch false gospel in which your assurance is based upon your conditional *performance* rather than Christ's unconditional *promises* will eventually leave you disillusioned, bitter and burnt out. You may be able to fake it for a long while (many Christians do) but you will eventually crash!

I get frustrated when I smell hints of legalistic manipulation in the preaching of some pastors and Christian leaders. One of the reasons for my irritation is that I was once held captive to such techniques from religious celebrities I looked up to! Anyone can manipulate a crowd, but as a pastor myself, I want my teaching to *motivate* rather than *manipulate*. The truth is that only an epiphany of grace – the experiential embrace of God's absolute, unconditional and irreversible kindness offered to us in Christ – will motivate us toward allowing Him to live His supernatural life through us.

Incidentally, after Paul encourages believers not to allow sin to dominate them (Romans 6), he then candidly shares about his own struggle to live by a righteous standard of behavior (Romans 7). Consider some of the things Paul confesses:

> (14) We know that the law is spiritual, but I am unspiritual, sold as a slave to sin. (15) I do not understand what I do. For what I want to do I do not do, but what I hate I do....

> (18) I know that nothing good lives in me, that is, in my sinful nature (literally "flesh"). For I have the desire to do what is good, but I cannot carry it out. (19) For what I do is not the good I want to do; no, the evil I do not want to do – this I keep on doing...

> (21) So I find this law and work: When I want to do good, evil is right there with me.

Having read those words, can you imagine virtually *any* spiritual leader being so candid about personal struggles in today's religious climate? Picture Paul being interviewed for a leadership position by just about *any* modern-day church or ministry. I can almost hear the conversation now...

> **Search Committee:** So tell us a bit about your spiritual life, Paul...

> **Paul:** Uh, well, much of the time I feel like a walking bundle of paradoxes. I really want to do what is right, but often I end up doing the exact opposite. I feel like a complete failure sometimes! Even though I delight in obeying God, I often feel

these dark, primal tendencies that seem like they're running through my veins. I'm pretty miserable when this happens, if you really want to know the truth.

Search Committee: Umm, okay then, thanks for your time, Paul. Don't call us – we'll call you…

You get the point! The Apostle that deals most thoroughly with the themes of sin, grace, salvation and righteous living is also the guy who most honestly portrays the believer's struggle by way of his own confession. When we read Romans, we never get the sense that we should simply "accept sin". Yet, we are *repeatedly* encouraged to accept our unconditional standing and identity in Christ, seeking to be as patient with our growth process as He is. We have no right to preach about a compassionate God if we are not willing to learn compassion toward ourselves!

Brennan Manning rightly identifies four major roadblocks that can paralyze us along the path toward authentic life-transformation. These obstacles, Manning argues, are *projectionism, perfectionism, moralism/legalism,* and *unhealthy guilt.*[44] I will attempt to briefly illuminate these concepts as follows…

Projectionism

Projectionism is that tendency in many of us to "project onto God" our own existential feelings about what He might be like and how we think He must view us, especially in our worst moments. Many influences – from childhood experiences to family origins to teachers and religious leaders – can impact the way we relate to God. While not all of these influences are necessarily harmful or inaccurate, certainly many can be.

Manning suggests that our projection is a "process of unwittingly ascribing to God our own attitudes and feelings as an unconscious defense of our own inadequacy and guilt."[45] Only grace sets us free to measure our understanding of God against His ultimate revelation of Himself – the Person of Jesus. All pre-conceived notions of God must be tested in light of the Person of Jesus Christ. This means that if ever our picture of God conflicts with the qualities revealed in the character of Jesus – we must by grace, cast those inaccurate assumptions aside as the idolatry that they are.

Perfectionism

Secondly, there is the debilitating problem of perfectionism. While Manning insightfully describes the perfectionist as a person who is "locked into the saint-or-sinner syndrome, tyrannized by an all-or-nothing mentality"[46], author and pastor David Seamands adds that perfectionism "is the most disturbing emotional problem among evangelical Christians."[47]

Seamands argues that through obsessive feelings of failure, self-deprecation, anxiety and other symptoms, perfectionism strangles the believer from ever resting in the reality that God's grace truly is enough! As a pastor and fellow believer, I can vouch for the reality that far too many Christians struggle with the issue of perfectionism!

Moralism / Legalism

If Seamonds is correct that perfectionism is the most "disturbing" problem among Christians, I would argue that moralism and legalism are the most pervasive. These are at the core of what motivates the various types of front-loading and back-loading theology I sought to confront in the first section of this book.

Moralizing is when "personal responsibility to an inviolable moral code replaces personal response to God's loving call," Manning notes. "Moralism and its stepchild, legalism, reduce the love story of God for his people to the observance of burdensome religious duties and oppressive laws."[48]

This leads to a few key questions:

- Do you ever feel more "approved of" by God when you sense that things are "going well" in your moral behavior or spiritual "commitments"?

- Do you feel as though God is more "pleased" with you after having your morning devotions or giving to charity?

- Have you ever struggled with that aggressive, nagging sense of God's disapproval we addressed previously?

If so, it is likely that you do not understand the grace of God as it is freely offered through Jesus Christ. It is likely that you struggle with the age-old cancer of legalism. Do you remember what we learned about legalism in chapter 1?

Legalism is *any attitude or belief that human merit can produce, prove or preserve for oneself an acceptable standing before God*. If you struggle with this, you are not alone. Legalism is the most pervasive roadblock to real spiritual growth – and the building blocks of legalism are rooted deeply in the opening story of the Hebrew Scriptures.

In Genesis 3, after Adam and Eve had "fallen" into sin before God, we immediately observe behaviors which are no less common for us than for them. As they "sewed fig leaves together" to cover their nakedness, we realize that this scene is depicting their shame. After innocence was lost, they felt disgusted with themselves for the first time, and they attempted to remedy the problem on their own terms.

As we noted previously, the story accentuates the love and mercy of God when we are made aware of Yahweh's response. Rather than reacting venomously toward these disoriented humans we see God graciously perform the first animal sacrifice (an obvious shadow of things to come) and cover their nakedness *on His own terms* with the garments of fur.

As the Biblical narrative unfolds, the veiled symbolism becomes clearer as we realize that essentially God is saying, "You cannot fix yourself! You must come to me on *my* terms – not yours. My terms are terms of grace and unrelenting mercy whereby *I provide the sacrifice and I do the fixing* – not you." This gentle grace is God's initial response to the original sin of His creatures, and it is His consistent offer to humanity throughout the ages up through the present day!

Unhealthy Guilt:

Finally, there is the reality of unhealthy guilt. Some will argue, *"Wait a minute! Doesn't God use guilt in a positive way to keep our behavior in check?"* That depends upon your definition of the terms. God *does* create us with a conscience by which He alerts us to our need for reasonable self-examination and humility. He has also given us the Holy Spirit as our Counselor to guide us into truth.

However, the goal of this kind of so-called "guilt" is never to invoke shame, but to stimulate *agreement with God* (the literal meaning of confession) about the truth that His path is always best for us and for the world. The Bible describes this reality as a "godly sorrow that leads to repentance."[49]

The unhealthy guilt Manning warns of is a crippling reality for far too many children of God. I would describe this unhealthy guilt as synonymous with "shame". Whereas a spiritually and emotionally healthy conscience allows us to honestly admit and assess where we have gone wrong, shame paralyzes us with hysteric feelings of unlovableness and rejection before God and others. While the conscience and the Holy Spirit help a believer realize and admit, "I have behaved wrongly," shame deceives that person with the paralyzing notion that "I *am* wrong. Something about me is *unusually* flawed and *particularly unworthy* of grace."

Making the Good News too Good?

The great news about grace is that – when understood, believed and embraced – it is able to confront and dismantle these cancerous roadblocks to spiritual vitality and authentic joy of living. Grace stares shame in the face and refuses to argue with it.

Instead grace says to shame, "You are correct. This person *is* unworthy. This person *is* flawed. This person *is* deserving of punishment. And *that* is why I'm here! This is the entire point of my existence! By definition, I am totally unearned, unmerited and unable to be lost once obtained! And those are the very reasons, Mr. Shame, that *I win* and *you lose*."

The bottom line is that you will never surrender to a God you don't fully trust. Begging and groveling at the feet of the Almighty is neither surrender *nor* confession, yet this is the way countless believers relate to God on a daily basis. Because we have such little trust in the unconditional reliability of His promises, we somehow feel that self-deprecation, begging for forgiveness and verbalizing how pathetic we are will convince Him to extend His grace for just a bit longer. This is not the invitation Jesus was making when He said, "Come to me, all you who are weary and heavy burdened…and I will give you rest." (Matthew 11:28)

Front-loaders of the gospel would have you believe that living a righteous life will *ensure* your salvation. Back-loaders seek to convince you that good works will *assure* you of your salvation. Both undermine the unique message of the uncut gospel of grace! These teachers often claim that the reason many Christians live lives dominated by sin is because the grace of God has been made *too* opportunistic. In essence, they claim say we've made it *too* free and easy!

Might I suggest that the exact *opposite* is true? The reality is that we have *failed* to esteem grace to the level that God Himself esteems it. By front-loading and back-loading, bait-and-switch fear tactics and manipulative strategies to "keep people in line", we have neutered the gospel of its unique power!

Only the unconditional reliability of grace can motivate a person to truly fruitful living. Only when I am assured that it is impossible for me to fall beyond God's grip can I then learn to walk in freedom from the grip of sin with increasing measure. This inarguable fact can be illustrated by a feat of engineering located less than one hour from where I live.

The Practical Power of Grace

Between 1933 and 1937, thousands of workers were employed to construct the world-famous Golden Gate Bridge in San Francisco, California. Up until that time, bridge-building was a ruthless profession which claimed the lives of countless workers who fell to their deaths in projects across the nation and around the world. The

Golden Gate project, however, employed a different strategy which proved to be more than worth its weight in gold.

Project managers decided to stretch a reinforced massive net below the workers, spanning across the entire workspace. What was so great about this safety net is that it allowed the workers to focus more clearly on their challenging tasks. At a time when bridge-building was known on average for taking one human life for every one million dollars spent on a bridge project, there were only 11 lives lost on the $35 million Golden Gate project. What is more amazing is that this figure would have been confined to only *one* lost life if it hadn't been for an entire scaffold that fell, tearing through the net and killing 10 men in one tragic accident!

The point becomes obvious when you begin to think about it. Thousands of workers – employed by ten primary contractors and all of their subs – were able to produce what was at the time the longest suspension bridge in world history. And they completed the Golden Gate in the astonishingly short window of only four years! Why? *Because the workers knew that they had a reliable safety net beneath them.* When their fears of plunging to their deaths below were eliminated, they were able to work more efficiently than the vast majority of those gone before them.

This, among many other things, is what grace accomplishes for us. It frees us from being overly focused on making mistakes. It frees us to rest in the reality that we can never fall beyond the eternal security of God's rescuing power. For this reason the Apostle of love encouraged his audience with the reassuring words

> My dear children, I write these things to you so that you will not sin. But if anyone does sin, we have an advocate with the Father, Jesus Christ the righteous one.[50]

Is it possible for grace to be taken advantage of? Absolutely! By definition, grace is open to the possibility of abuse. There is simply no way around it. Yet this did not prevent God from offering His grace. Only when grace is freely taught and fully understood, will the abuser eventually come to his or her senses and surrender to the compassion of the Father and the freedom of the Spirit!

The Corinthian Case Study

In his excellent book *Stripped: Uncensored Grace on the Streets of Las Vegas*, pastor Jud Wilhite makes a notable comparison between ancient Corinth and the culture his own church seeks to impact in "Sin City".[51] He notes that Corinth was a large, booming port community which prided itself in being one of the cutting-edge cultural centers of the Greco-Roman world.

Filled with artists, scientists, commerce and education, it was the home of the Isthmian Games (a precursor to the Olympics) and was known for a bustling transient population. Complete with its equivalent of pubs, clubs and hotels, Corinth was also a hotbed of unrestrained sexual expression, much of which would make today's mainstream America look rather tame.

As one might expect, much of the hedonism in that culture had also found its way into the fledgling new churches Paul had planted in the region. Much of First Corinthians is directed toward confronting behaviors such as divisiveness, tolerance of unsound teaching, incest and adultery, lawsuits between church members, rampant divorce, chaotic worship gatherings, misuse of spiritual gifts, and the list goes on. In spite of all this, Paul nevertheless refers to the Corinthians with such terms as "sanctified", "brothers and sisters", "dear friends", the "body" of Christ, etc.

These people were struggling, to say the least, in their quest to live holy lives. They were Christians who had received the uncut gospel, but they were still trapped by many familiar sins, habits and attachments. You could say that they were anything *but* surrendered to the Lordship of Christ in their lives. Paul was certainly strong and passionate when he addressed their sin, but he was never less than gracious in affirming their legitimacy as partakers of God's saving grace.

Paul clearly seemed to know what many modern-day church leaders either forget or deny: God's kindness (His expressed grace) leads people to repentance.[52] Our minds and hearts start to change when we begin to actualize the *unconditional* nature of God's goodness toward us in Christ. This is the only real plane on which lasting transformation happens.

But What About Fruit-Bearing?

Fruit-bearing is a concept that Christians use in reference to a tour of a vineyard Jesus gave to His disciples just hours before His arrest and crucifixion. Using the fields full of grapevines as His object lesson, Jesus said

> I am the vine; you are the branches. If a man remains (abides, lives, rests) in me and I in him, he will bear much fruit; apart from me you can do nothing.[53]

In context, Jesus was in the process of sharing with His followers exactly what discipleship would look like under the provisions of the New Covenant He was about to inaugurate. Following Him would be about abiding in Him as the Vine, depending upon the Holy Spirit to produce spiritual "fruit" in their lives.

This was a radically different approach to discipleship than the other ancient Rabbis could offer to their disciples. An ordinary Rabbi could say to his students, "Try to imitate the way I live my life." By contrast, Jesus was saying, "There is only one Person who can really live the Christian life. The only way you can truly follow me is to allow me to live my life *through* you like sap flows from the vine into the branches to produce grapes."

The Apostle Paul would further develop this New Covenant way of discipleship when He emphasized that "the fruit of the Spirit is love, joy, peace, patience, kindness, goodness, faithfulness, gentleness and self control."[54] We'll take a closer look at New Covenant discipleship in the final chapter, but for now I want to address those who might still assume that proponents of the uncut gospel tend to minimize the importance of godly living.

One of the admitted weaknesses of the early "free grace"

movement I referred to in the first part of this book was simply that some proponents seemed to imply that a person could claim to receive Christ by faith and then walk away from Him or even completely reject Him without ever casting doubt upon the legitimacy of their salvation. I want to be clear that I am *not* arguing for such a position in this book.

Every believer in Jesus will bear *some* kind of spiritual fruit, whether it is obviously recognizable or not. On this issue I agree with the free-grace proponent Dr. Joseph Dillow, who said

> Those who have been born again will always give some evidence of growth in grace and spiritual interest and commitment. A man who claims he is a Christian and yet never manifests any change at all has no reason to believe he is justified.[55]

Another leading proponent of the free grace position with whom I agree on this point, Dr. Charles Ryrie, also affirms

> Every Christian will bear spiritual fruit. Somewhere, sometime, somehow. Otherwise that person is not a believer. Every born-again individual will be fruitful. Not to be fruitful is to be faithless, without faith, and therefore without salvation.[56]

While standing in total agreement with the statements above, I also agree with their teachings about the fact that fruit can be nearly impossible to quantify. For example, as a pastor I may counsel with a believer who struggles with a recurring abuse of alcohol. From the outside looking in, another person who knows of this man's constant battle may judgmentally conclude that if he were *truly* a Christian, he would eventually overcome this addiction. On the surface, it doesn't seem like much fruit is evident in his life.

What the casual observer may *not* see, however, is the fact that this man cries himself to sleep many nights over the pain this is causing himself and his family. The casual observer may not realize this person is reaching out for pastoral care or Christ-centered therapy. The casual observer merely sees the surface and is tempted to make a judgment based on this man's struggle, while not understanding that *the struggle itself is in fact fruit!*

Have you ever thought about your struggles this way? Have you ever realized that often your struggles themselves *are* fruit, bearing witness to the fact that you *are* indeed a genuine child of God?

Think about it. The Bible teaches that it is the *nature* of an unbeliever to sin. Most Christians I talk to will admit that before they became believers, they hardly cared about sin, if at all. Some didn't even believe in the concept of sin.

A non-believer may even lay awake at night inventing new ways to sin without ever questioning that propensity within themselves. Why? Because before we receive Christ, *sinfulness is our nature.* Prior to spiritual re-birth, we are doing exactly what our nature dictates. There is no real spiritual struggle that we are aware of. Oh sure, we may feel bad about the consequences our sin brings to us or to those we love, but it is not a spiritual battle for us because the knowledge of Christ eludes us until salvation.

When we become believers in Christ, we inherit a *brand new nature* that is completely surrendered to and compatible with the Spirit of God. This is what 2 Corinthians 5:17 means when Paul says, "Therefore, if anyone is in Christ, he is a new creation; the old has gone, the new has come!"

In the case of the believer abusing alcohol, his conflict runs much deeper than merely the pain of earthly consequences. That may be *part* of the equation, but for alcoholic, it's a conflict of identity because he knows who he really is at the core of his being but he is living to please the flesh…and he hates it.

The casual observer may spitefully judge this man's heart, but a such judgment is not for any human to make, since the man's struggle itself is indeed a very real kind of fruit. If the Spirit were not alive in this man's life, there would likely be no struggle in the first place beyond self-focused regret over personal consequences.

Casual about Carnality?

The term "carnality" is a Christian term referring to the habit of gratifying the sinful desires of the "flesh" (more on that later). By affirming the existence of "carnal Christians" I am not in any way suggesting that this is a *preferable* way to live the Christian life. I'm only affirming that it is *possible*. If it weren't, it is highly unlikely that Paul would have invested so much effort in teaching the early churches how to overcome the flesh. I argued for this already in part one of this book.

Certainly it is possible for a genuine believer to be living in blatant, willful rebellion against God. No matter how "happy" this person appears on the outside, they will inevitably suffer some sort of earthly consequence as a result of continued carnality. This is simply the truth of reaping what we sow and it is true in the natural realm whether a person is a believer or not.

In reality, spiritual immaturity, carnality and a lack of apparent fruit can be related to many different things, such as bad theological teaching, abusive religious environments and other forms of spiritual malnourishment. As a father of three young boys, if I gave two of them nourishing food and plenty of exercise while limiting the other to junk food and video games, it is fairly obvious which one would look and act the most unhealthy by adulthood.

The truth is obvious: carnal Christians *do* exist and the fruit that they bear may be buried under the evidence of mal-nutrition to the point that they are almost indistinguishable from the world. The fact that this is the case is, again, the very reason why the authors of the New Covenant letters spent so much time seeking to lead believers out of their worldliness.

> To believe in the existence of carnal Christians, then, does not suggest that we are being casual about carnality.

To believe in the existence of carnal Christians, then, does not suggest that we are being casual about carnality. As a father, pastor and believer in Jesus, I mince no words in seeking to warn people about the foolishness of choosing sin over the Spirit. But I will not deny what the Scripture clearly teaches in order to try to manipulate people into greater "surrender to Christ's Lordship." We don't "make Jesus Lord" of our lives. *He is Lord*, period!

As a believer, I can choose to walk by the Spirit, thus affirming His Lordship – or I can choose to walk by the flesh and risk the consequence of ending up miserable in this life. Either way, I am proving that Jesus is Lord and that His ways are always the best choice. These choices have nothing to do with whether or not I will go to heaven when I die, but they are deeply connected to the abundant life I can enjoy while on this earth.

Chapter 8: Myths and Legends

T hus far in our journey we have discovered that there are front-loaders of the gospel who try to insert preliminary *requirements* into the front-end of the deal. We have also learned about back-loaders who attach all kinds of mandatory *results* to the backside of the gospel, making such claims as, "If you are *truly* saved, your life better look like this or that…"

We were reminded from Hebrews 10 that whenever our assurance and security rests upon *our performance* rather than upon *Christ's promises* – we are in for a spiritual train-wreck filled with fear, depression and anxiety. So many Christians – genuine believers in Christ – live their lives under a cloudy, oppressive sense of God's constant disapproval.

The transformation of our minds – spoken of in Romans 12:1-3 – is rarely an overnight process. When we have subtly believed lies and half-truths that have taken years to compound inside of us – it usually takes some time to walk out from under the influence of those fairy tales.

> When we have subtly believed lies and half-truths that have taken years to compound inside of us – it usually takes some time to walk out from under the influence of those fairy tales.

By now you understand that the uncut gospel is not about *front-loading* or *back-loading*. In reality, the gospel is about *free*loading! It is about surrendering to the reality that you and I bring absolutely *nothing* but trust to the equation – and that Jesus *alone* is enough.

To make this assertion inevitably provokes a series of questions related to various *myths and legends* we may have picked up over the course of time. Those questions often relate to the relationship between faith and works. In this chapter we will consider three of the most common myths Christians believe.

We will begin with a famous passage found in Matthew 6:12-15 in the middle of Jesus' Sermon on the Mount. Many believers are familiar with at least some of these words – because they are part of what we commonly call "The Lord's Prayer" or the "Our Father". It is because of this passage of Scripture that some folks are inclined to believe the first of these myths…

MYTH #1: As Christians, we should pray for God to forgive us of our sins

Among other things, Matthew 6:12-15 records Jesus teaching His disciples to pray the following:

> *Forgive us our debts* (sins), as we also have forgiven our debtors. And lead us not into temptation, but deliver us from the evil one. For if you forgive men when they sin against you, your heavenly Father will also forgive you. But *if you do not forgive men their sins, your Father will not forgive your sins.*

Like the Hebrews 10 passage we discussed in chapter 4, these verses in Matthew 6 once played serious games with my head! After all, the words seem to contain such a huge contradiction! Out of one side of their mouths, I would hear preachers talk about how God's forgiveness is an unconditionally free gift. But out of the other side, I would hear them employ all sorts of mental gymnastics in order to explain this passage away.

In this Scripture, Jesus seems to clearly state that in order for God to forgive us, we first need to forgive others. If we don't, then apparently God won't forgive us! This doesn't sound like an unconditional offer of forgiveness, does it? As if you didn't know by now, I will remind you again with regard to the content of the Sermon on the Mount that Jesus' words were spoken within a specific historical and theological context that we must carefully pay attention to.

A lot of us have "red-letter" versions of the Bible, where all of Christ's words are highlighted in *red* lettering. The Bible I most often read is like that, and while I think it's a great feature, we have to be aware of at least one subtle message it can send.

The assumption we are sometimes led to make is that the red letters are *more* important or significant than other parts of Scripture simply because they were spoken directly from Christ's mouth as He walked the earth. The problem with this idea becomes obvious when we consider that Paul declared that *all* Scripture is God-breathed and is equally the inspired Word of God. And while Christ's words recorded in the Gospels are indeed precious to us, they are not *more* important or authoritative than any other part of the inspired text.

In essence, the entire Bible is the Word of Jesus. The Holy Spirit inspired the text of Scripture from Genesis to Revelation. So in reality – the words recorded by Moses *are* the words of the eternal Christ. The words of the prophets *are* the words of the eternal Christ. The words of Paul and the other Apostles *are* all equally the words of the eternal Christ.

Not only must we be careful about making these false-differentiations with God's Word – but I continue to emphasize that Jesus' words were given in a specific historical narrative, to a specific audience, with a specific purpose in mind. What is more, the human author had specific intentions in building his narrative in order to make a specific argument to a specific group of readers. Herein lies the challenge of accurate hermeneutics (interpretation) of Scripture.

Having said all of that, I will further reiterate that it is important to realize the teachings of Jesus were articulated in a very transitional time period, toward the end of the Old System-era. They were pointing

His audience toward the New System that would soon be inaugurated through His death, burial and resurrection.

Even though the words of Christ are recorded in what we consider to be the New Testament (according to how our Bibles are organized) it is crucial to understand that the New Covenant did not begin until Jesus actually died and rose again. As we've already discussed, this means that Jesus' entire ministry occurred under the *old system* up until the cross and the empty tomb!

There are a lot of things Jesus said and did that are impossible to reconcile with the promises of the New Covenant. When we understand the reality of Him ministering under the Old Covenant, much of this confusion lifts away. Jesus said *many* things that are simply incompatible with the New Covenant, and this is because He was pointing people to their need for this New Covenant which had not yet been instituted at the time. For example, you might remember the story of the Rich Young Man from Matthew 19.

He came to Jesus and asked "What must I *do* to receive eternal life?" And how did Jesus respond? He said "Keep the commandments." Now let me ask you as a Christian, is *that* what you would tell someone who asked you the same question? Of course not! You would never tell a person that eternal life could be obtained by keeping the Law. Even the most basic understanding of the gospel of grace would prohibit you from doing that.

The dialogue continued as the rich man basically responded, "I have kept all the commandments! What else is there to do?" And Jesus essentially replied, "Okay, but if you want to be perfect, go sell all your possessions and give the money to the poor, and you will have treasure in Heaven."

The story goes on to tell us that the rich young man went away in sadness because he had great wealth. What was Jesus' point? His point is found in the way He answered the question.

Remember, the young man asked about *how* to have eternal life – and specifically, what he had to *do* to gain it. But Jesus responded, "If you want to be *perfect*, go sell your possessions…" Jesus knew the very thing this man struggled with. It was a form of greed that the man himself was not yet aware of. Jesus is essentially saying "If you want eternal life, you've got to be *perfect* by perfectly keeping the demands of the law!"

Jesus was intentionally driving this man – and everyone else who would hear or read about this encounter – to despair. He did this so that His audience would have no other alternative than to consider receiving eternal life as a *free gift* on the basis of grace through faith alone.

Jesus would frequently use the Law for the very purpose that the Apostle Paul said it was made for. The Law was never given so that we could find salvation by keeping it. It was precisely the opposite! Paul said that the law was given in order to prove to us our incapability of keeping it, thereby driving us to the foot of the cross to receive the *free gift* of forgiveness, life and righteousness by *grace*! (Rom. 7:7).

> Paul said that the law was given in order to prove to us our incapability of keeping it, thereby driving us to the foot of the cross to receive the *free gift* of forgiveness, life and righteousness by *grace*!

We already discussed in chapter 1 that in the Sermon on the Mount, Jesus elevated the Law to an even *higher* standard than was commonly understood. Again, Jesus said to His audience that unless their righteousness *surpassed* that of the Pharisees, they wouldn't have the slightest hope of entering into God's Kingdom! We also learned that the main point of the Sermon on the Mount was *not* about giving Christians a higher standard of living to aim for! The point was to drive religious Jews (and other legalists who might come along after them) to the reality that *no one* can measure up to God's Holy standards no matter how hard they might try!

That was also the major point of numerous statements Jesus made as He was pointing people to faith in His impending death on the cross. If you've ever read the Sermon on the Mount and felt like a total loser – you actually *get* it! That's the whole point of the sermon – that in and of ourselves we are totally helpless and lost, unable to attain to the perfection demanded by God's standards – no matter how moral or deserving we think we are!

Now back to our passage at hand. The fact that Jesus puts a *condition* on God's forgiveness here in Matthew 6 is not an attempt to suggest that we can perfectly carry out this command! Instead, He was ministering under the Old Covenant and pointing His thoroughly Jewish audience toward grasping their need for the New. In essence He was saying, "You'd better just give up! You simply *cannot* – on your *best* day – be *good enough* to meet God's requirement, because the standard is absolute, total, perfection!" If you fail to live up to even one point of God's standard (in this case, forgiving the sins of others), you are disqualified!

We also learned previously that this essentially leaves us with one of two options: try harder to be perfect – or give up by surrendering to the grace. For years, I was held hostage by the "try harder" theory. In reality, the uncut gospel is not about "trying harder". Ironically, it's about "giving up!" It's about throwing in the towel and waiving the white flag of surrender so that Jesus can live His supernatural life through us! What a crucial difference this subtle shift in our understanding can make!

This truth brings a new richness to Jesus' words on the cross when He said "Father, forgive them, for they know not what they do." Think about that! In Jesus' worst hour of pain and torment – He offered the very forgiveness that Matthew 6:14-15 demands of *us*. This is one of many examples of how Jesus *fulfilled* God's lawful requirements on our behalf.

He carried out the commandments perfectly in our place because He knew we would not. He lived this life in utter perfection because you and I could not. That is why the Bible calls Jesus our *substitute*. He lived the life we couldn't live, paid the debt for our sin that we couldn't pay, and then supernaturally transferred *His* righteousness to *our* spiritual bank account based on simply receiving the gift by grace through faith!

Supplement or Substitute?

Unfortunately, many Christians think of Jesus as a *supplement* rather than a *substitute*! They reason that by "adding some Jesus" to their lives, they can hope to become a better person. But they forget that Jesus didn't come to make naughty people nice. He came to make dead people alive!

So in relation to Matthew 6:12-15, Jesus is intentionally painting a very bleak scenario for his listeners. Jesus says that in the same manner we judge others or fail to offer forgiveness, it will be returned to us. But more amazing still is that by the end of Jesus' life, we see Him actually *fulfilling* the very standard of perfection that we were utterly incapable of measuring up to – even going so far as to articulate forgiveness toward those who were in the very act of crucifying Him as He spoke the words, "Father, forgive them…"

He didn't give us this warning about our need to forgive as perfectly as God forgives because He actually thought we could somehow *attain* to that level of perfection by trying really hard! Instead, He gave the warning in order to show us how infinitely high God's standard is – so that we would have no choice but to surrender in utter desperation to grace alone as our only means of meeting the standard! Jesus is not teaching works-based forgiveness. He is revealing a sinner's desperation for grace! And this leads us to reconsider another great myth we often believe…

MYTH #2: As Christians we must confess our sins in order to receive God's forgiveness.

In response to the truth revealed about Myth #1, people will naturally ask, *"What about confession of sin? Specifically, what about the famous 1 John 1:9 passage?"* Perhaps you have heard or read the verse: "If we confess our sins, He is faithful and just and will forgive us our sins and purify us from all unrighteousness."

I focused on this verse for the better part of two decades of following Jesus, mostly as a promise that I *believed* but didn't really understand. Perhaps you can see where the confusion comes from.

If I am already *totally* forgiven for my past, present and future sins by the blood of Christ – then why do I need to confess my sin in order to receive forgiveness? And if that were the case, then why does John write the following words only a few verses later in chapter 2:12: "I write to you, dear children, because your sins *have been forgiven* on account of his name"?

How do we explain this apparent contradiction? 1 John 1:9 seems to say that our confession somehow "triggers" God's forgiveness when our behavior falls short of His standard. But chapter 2 affirms along with many other New Testament passages that we *have already been* forgiven – past tense, once for all. Either we *already are* forgiven, or there is a condition for us to be *repeatedly forgiven*, but it can't be both. As always, this is yet another passage where context means everything!

Two Streams of Forgiveness?

In order to try to reconcile this apparent contradiction, I once believed and taught that there must be two different types or "streams" of forgiveness in view here. I reasoned that on the one hand, Christians are eternally forgiven in the *judicial* sense, meaning that God has wiped our sin out of the heavenly record-books.

On the other hand, I believed there was an ongoing need to *confess* sin in order to maintain what I called close "fellowship" with God. In other words, there was one sense in which I was forgiven *positionally* forever. But there was another sense in which I needed to be forgiven *practically* on an ongoing basis in order to stay "close" to God relationally. Pastor Andrew Farley humorously refers to this view of 1 John 1:9 the Christian's spiritual "bar of soap" method for maintaining daily fellowship with God.[57]

The major problem with this interpretation is that when we look at the text carefully, there is not even a *hint* of the notion that ongoing confession triggers additional forgiveness from God. Additionally, there is nothing else written in the New Testament to support that idea. It's a nice thought process. It sounds like a convenient way to synchronize an apparent contradiction, but the task we are concerned with is not about trying to make a contradiction sound more sensible or logical. What we care about is what the Bible is actually saying!

Most theologians would agree that it is not wise to base a major theological persuasion around one debatable verse. As Dr. Farley points out…

> "No other verse in the epistles appears to place a conditional 'if' on forgiveness and cleansing. So if there was a method for maintaining daily cleansing, the Romans were apparently unaware of it. If there was a prescription for keeping short accounts with God, the Galatians seemed to have had no exposure to it. If there was a need to ask God for forgiveness, the Ephesians were apparently not privy to it. Similarly, the Corinthians, Philippians, Colossians and Thessalonians also seemed to have missed this teaching."[58]

In an honest effort to take a closer look at the historical context of this letter, we must admit to some basic realities. During the latter part of the first century – after the other Apostles had been martyred – the elderly Apostle John was writing this letter to combat a series of false teachings that were finding their way into the local churches he was pastoring.

Who is John Speaking To?

Some of these false teachings were the foundation of what would eventually become known as Gnosticism. Gnostics had a *dualistic* view of spirituality. Among other things, these early Gnostics taught that…

1) The spiritual realm was good and pure
2) The material realm was evil and corrupt

What these pre-Gnostic teachers were saying was that because all matter is evil, Jesus could not have really come in human flesh. They claimed that He only *appeared* to have real flesh, but that this was just an illusion and that He was an entirely spiritual being.

This false teaching is the reason John begins this letter the way he does, seeking to assure both believers *and* non-believers that the Gnostic teachings about Christ's humanity were in fact *false*. He says the following about Jesus in verse 1 of the letter.

> That which was from the beginning, *which we have heard, which we have seen with our eyes, which we have looked at and our hands have touched* – this we proclaim to you concerning the Word of life.

In order to combat this Gnostic heresy that Jesus was not really a man, John boldly affirms "Oh yes He was! We *saw* Him, we *heard* Him, we *touched* Him with our own hands! To believe otherwise is a lie!" Later in the letter John re-emphasizes this point when he says that anyone who does not believe Jesus came in human flesh is "not from God" (1 John 4:3).

Today, we take it for granted that Jesus was a physical being. In fact, almost nobody denies that Jesus was a real historic figure. What people are more inclined to deny in our day is the claim that He was truly God.

With regard to our passage in question, it was the result of this dualistic thinking that led the Gnostics to believe that since the physical body was evil, there was really no such thing as "sin" in terms of nature or behavior. This became a second major falsehood that the group was promoting in the churches of Asia Minor.

Confronted by the infiltration of these heresies, John was doing what any good pastor would do – warning his flock not to believe this false teaching. It is in light of this warning to both believers *as well as* those who were embracing Gnostic dualism, that we discover that 1 John 1:9 is *not* directed toward believers – but to the Gnostics who had infiltrated their ranks to influence the churches.

Obviously, true believers in Christ do not claim that Jesus lacked a physical body. So in his opening statements of the letter, John is *not* principally addressing Christians. His words would have been *reaffirming* to Christians, but he is directly addressing the Gnostics themselves. That is why, after establishing that Jesus indeed had a material body, John writes in verse 8 that "If we claim to be without sin, we deceive ourselves and the truth is not in us."

Clearly, John is concerned with people who are claiming they are sinless. Do you know any Bible-believing Christian who claims he or she is sinless? Of course not! By definition, a person becomes a Christian by first admitting their sinfulness and dire need of Jesus to save them from sin! Someone making claims of sinlessness is by definition *not* a Christian – which again, was exactly the claim the Gnostics were making.

They were saying "There's no such thing as sin. Matter is evil anyway, so live and let live! Our spirits are safe with God and that's all that matters." In light of this we can more clearly see that John's opening words of the letter were intended to confront those two major false teachings: that *Jesus was non-physical* (1:1-4) and that *sin is a non-reality* (1:5-10)!

In light of this background we can easily see why 1 John 1:9 poses such confusion when we fail to read it in context. But some will still suggest that 1 John 1:9 *is* addressing Christians since the Apostle uses the pronoun "we," which makes it seem like he is including himself as a believer in the group he is addressing. Of course, if verse 9 was all we had, we might be led to believe that. Fortunately for us, God's Word is clear in this passage because this verse is sandwiched between two verses in which the pronouns "we" and "us" are clearly used for *unbelievers.*

In verse 8, John says, "If *we* claim to be without sin...the truth is not in *us*". In verse 10, John continues, "If *we* claim *we* have not sinned...His Word is not in *us*." So the context reveals in a rather clear manner that John is not using the word "we" in terms of identifying himself with believers specifically – but rather with humanity in general – since as we already affirmed, verses 8 and 10 simply do not and cannot refer to Christians.

What 1 John 1:9 *is* communicating to these unbelieving Gnostics is that anyone who has bought into these heretical ideas of denying the existence of sin needs to become a Christian! Becoming a Christian begins by the admission of one's personal sinfulness and that through confession of that sinfulness, one can receive *by faith* the God who is faithful and just to forgive and cleanse them of *all unrighteousness*! John is saying that the answer to the sin problem is not to deny its reality – but to become a Christian, receiving by faith the unconditional forgiveness of a gracious and benevolent God!

The verb "to confess" literally means "to say the same thing as" or "to agree with." John is essentially saying, "You can either agree with falsehood or you can agree with God about your sinfulness and need for a Savior!"

And did you also notice that the promise is that God will cleanse them from *all* unrighteousness? All means *all* – and unlike the "bar of soap" understanding I alluded to earlier, this contextual interpretation is totally consistent with the dozens of other unconditional forgiveness passages in the New Testament epistles!

The Accurate Conclusion

1 John 1:9 is not intended to condone a one-by-one tallying of our sins so that we can confess them in order to find ongoing forgiveness or maintain "closeness" with God. When we have placed our faith in the once-for-all sacrifice of Jesus Christ, we are *totally* and *eternally* forgiven. Because of the uncut gospel of grace, we are irreversibly close to God regardless of our behavioral performance.

> Because of the uncut gospel of grace, we are irreversibly close to God regardless of our behavioral performance.

What a tragedy that so many of us – including myself for many years – have been taught to dialogue with God in order to *feel* closer, more forgiven and cleansed by Him as though some spiritual transaction were taking place over and over again! Historically, many Christians have used 1 John 1:9 in desperation in order to feel closer to God when in reality, this concept is foreign to the New Covenant!

For some of us, such an epiphany is a hard pill to swallow! It can feel very disconcerting to admit that one of our long-held beliefs is not as Biblical as we once thought. Let me be clear that for the believer confession itself is by no means *wrong* or *unbiblical,* so long as we understand what confession does and does not mean and what it does and does not accomplish.

As we have learned, to "confess" means "to agree or say the same thing as". As Believers, we should be willing to agree with God about everything – including our sinful behavior. And while we should never think of confession in terms of a way to gain or receive ongoing forgiveness from God, it is definitely appropriate for us to agree with God concerning the foolishness of our sins.

As Christians, confessing our sins to God is about humility – not forgiveness. We don't need to keep so-called "short accounts" with God. He has removed our sins – past, present and future – as far as the east is from the west! Miraculously, He doesn't remember them (Jer. 31:34; Heb. 10:17). They are gone forever because of the once-for-all sacrifice of Jesus' blood being poured out on the cross!

Enjoying the Package-Deal!

Because this reality can feel so shocking, allow me to explain how this understanding of confession plays out for me practically in my life. No longer do I place *any stock whatsoever* in asking God for forgiveness, because I know that forgiveness is already my eternal possession as a gift! Unbroken fellowship with God is already part of the "package-deal" of salvation Jesus purchased for me through His death and resurrection. Asking God for forgiveness is like Donald Trump asking for God to make him wealthy! You don't have to ask for what you already have.

The way I now approach confession is to simply *agree with God* about the foolishness of my sin. I admit to Him that my sin hurts me as well as others and that it fails to bring glory to His Name. Often I am sorrowful over the foolishness of my actions. The Apostle Paul wrote that there is a "godly sorry that brings repentance."[59] When I know I have sinned, I humbly admit that my sinful behavior is out of step with my new nature and identity in Him, and I ask Him to help me rest in His completed work.

Now here comes the best part! After agreeing with God about my sin, I begin *thanking Him* for the fact that this sinful act was already forgiven at the cross. Understanding these realities has literally transformed my practice of confession, changing the experience from a guilt-ridden begging session into a dynamic, worshipful encounter in which my conscious mind (and behavior) is realigned with the grace and truth of Jesus.

More than Mere Semantics

Having explained that, some might accuse me of nit-picking over semantics her, but that is simply not the case. This is not just about a subtle difference of opinion or understanding. This is one of the differences between the "try-harder-false-gospel" and the "it-is-finished" uncut gospel of the New Covenant! The gospel is better left uncut and un-tweaked, because God got it right the first time! He doesn't need us to add our human maintenance plans in order to maintain closeness with Him!

> The gospel is better left uncut and un-tweaked, because God got it right the first time! He doesn't need us to add our human maintenance plans in order to maintain closeness with Him!

The "try harder" gospel variations of front-loading and back-loading will leave you tired, frustrated and burned-out! Those versions are *not* the good news of what Jesus has accomplished for us. The "it-is-finished" gospel is the real gospel Jesus was pointing to when He spoke those precious words we have been emphasizing throughout this book: *"Come to me – all you who are weary and burdened – and you will find rest for your souls. Take my yoke upon you and learn from Me - for I am gentle and humble in heart. My yoke is easy and my burden is light."*[60]

Yet still the skeptic might retort: "Okay, but if confession means that I simply *agree with God* about my sin and then *rest* in His all-sufficient grace – might I be tempted to abuse His grace as a free license to sin as much as I want?"

Of course you might be tempted to abuse His grace!

We addressed this concern earlier in the book. If you are a normal human being (and you are) there will unquestionably be times when you are tempted to abuse God's grace. All sin ultimately boils down to abusing our freedoms in one form or another! Temptation itself is not sin! When Paul spoke about not abusing grace as a license to sin in Romans 6, he explained clearly what he meant.

Interestingly, he did not say "If you want to avoid abusing the grace of God, then you need to die to yourself, take up your cross and follow Jesus!" Jesus said those words *prior* to His finished work on the cross! But *after* the cross and resurrection, Paul says this in Romans 6:1: "In the same way, *count yourselves dead to sin* but alive to God in Christ Jesus."

Can you see why I am making such a fuss about this? Our dying with Jesus is a one-time occurrence that happens at the moment we place faith in Him at our conversion. In contrast, "counting" or literally "reckoning" ourselves dead to sin is a *repeated* act of faith whenever we forget it. It is choosing to accept by faith that we have *already* died with Christ – and that because of this fact, sin no longer has the right to reign over us! It is about *resting* in the finished work of Jesus Christ, who is restfully seated at God's right hand.

> ... "counting" or literally "reckoning" ourselves dead to sin is a *repeated* act of faith whenever we forget it. It is choosing to accept by faith that we have *already* died with Christ – and that because of this fact, sin no longer has the right to reign over us!

I recently heard a radio preacher passionately shout to his listeners that "Jesus commands us to come and die!" I thought to myself "Yes, Jesus said those words, but that was *before* the cross and resurrection!" Now we are invited to *count* ourselves – to *accept as fact by faith* – that our old, sinful nature is already dead and that our new nature is alive to God!

Furthermore, in Romans 6:14 Paul unveils another precious promise: "For sin shall not be your master, because you are not under law, but under grace."

That verse is not a commandment! It is a promise! And if it is a promise that Jesus is desiring for you to simply *rest* in by faith, then how do you see yourself at this very moment? Are you a person constantly in need of God's forgiveness – or totally forgiven? Are you a sinner saved by grace – or a saint resting in grace?

Yet still the push-back continues: *"Yes, but what about the conviction of the Holy Spirit? Isn't His job to convict us of sin so that we can turn away from it?"* I'm glad you asked, because that is a great segue into our third and final myth...

MYTH #3: As Christians, the Holy Spirit will convict us about our sin so that we turn from it

We use this jargon a lot – the idea that the Holy Spirit "convicts" us of our sin. Let me ask you a question: What is the root of the English term "conviction"? It is the noun "convict". And just what is a *convict* but someone who stands condemned for a crime?

Think carefully about this. We learned from Hebrews 10 that God remembers our sins no more. Now ask yourself, *"Who is the Holy Spirit?"* If you have been a Christian for any length of time, you know that the Holy Spirit is God Almighty – the third Divine Member of the Trinity along with the Father and Son. So how is it, then, that we imagine somehow that God the Father doesn't remember our sins anymore, but God the Holy Spirit does – and that it is His job to keep bringing that sin to our attention?

In John 16, Jesus says that one of the roles of the Holy Spirit is to convict the *world* of sin, righteousness and judgment, but nowhere in the New Testament is the Holy Spirit said to "convict" Christians! The idea of "convicting" literally means "to find guilty". The Holy Spirit does not declare guilt upon a person who has been washed forever clean by the blood of Christ! In relation to the Christian, the Scripture *does* ascribe to the Holy Spirit such designations as *Counselor, Comforter, Helper,* and *Advocate*. But never is it his job to make us feel guilty.

When sinful behavior occurs in our lives and we have that guilty feeling we interpret as "conviction" – such an impression is not to be confused with the activity of the Holy Spirit. That alarm is simply the inner realization that there is a battle going on between our New Identity and our *flesh*, which consists of our old selfish habits, patterns, weaknesses and coping mechanisms.

Feeling guilty when we've misbehaved is not an experience unique to Christians. God has woven a basic moral conscience into the fabric of all humanity. What *is* unique to Christians is how we *deal with* guilty feelings.

The Holy Spirit's job is not to convict believers of sin, but to *remind* us of the blood that Jesus shed for our sin. We don't need the Holy Spirit to feel guilty for doing something wrong! We need the Holy Spirit to remind us of the blood of Christ shed for our sins! We need Him to counsel us that there is a better way to live – and to comfort us with the fact that God will never give up on us even when we feel like giving up on ourselves! When Paul speaks of that "godly sorrow" which brings repentance to our lives[61], it is not to be used as a synonym for "conviction."

> We don't need the Holy Spirit to feel guilty for doing something wrong! We need the Holy Spirit to remind us of the blood of Christ shed for our sins!

In light of these three myths, are you becoming more convinced that there may be some religious assumptions you need to re-assess? Sunday after Sunday, Christians are bombarded with the perpetuation of myths like these and others. They may sound like technicalities – mere minor differences of opinion or application. But added together, they begin to spin a devastating web of religious bondage in the life of many believers. Unlearning these misconceptions is crucial to enjoying the freedom Jesus purchased for us!

Make no mistake about it – if you are a Christian through faith in Jesus Christ, you are permanently forgiven of all your sins, and the Holy Spirit will never rub your failure in your face. It is the internal experience of this kind of grace which enables us to respond with the external expressions of God's goodness so desperately needed in the world today. This is the practical power of the Gospel Uncut, which we will explore in the final section – *Unleash*.

PART THREE: (UN)LEASH -
Living in the Power of the Uncut Gospel

Chapter 9: Resting or Wrestling?

y own journey toward a deeper and more consistent experience of grace-based transformation (as opposed to religious behavior modification) has come about in a most paradoxical way. As I have embraced the reality that spiritual warfare has more to do with my *resting in Christ* than with my *wrestling with the Devil*, I have embarked upon a more joyous, Biblical path of spiritual growth.

In a fallen world, many of us struggle with a deep root of shame in our lives. By shame, I am not speaking of "guilt", as though the two are synonymous. I mentioned in chapter 7 that David Seamands explains the difference in a profound way. He affirms that while feelings of *guilt* can alert us to the fact that we have behaved wrongly in some way (perhaps inspiring us to make amends with someone we have sinned against), *shame* seeks to paralyze us with the feeling that *we* are particularly wrong, evil or crooked in some grossly abnormal way.[62]

Shame on You?

Shame causes us to believe that while all people struggle with sin, *our* particular struggles are especially heinous. These irrational but powerful feelings kept me in a cycle of religious bondage for years, as I compared myself to other believers who I viewed as more qualified or spiritual than me. Even today, I sometimes find my thoughts reverting back to a shame-based image of myself – especially when a sinful behavior has recently gotten the best of me.

For me, shame began to escalate noticeably during my pre-teen years. I was exposed to pornography by a 13 year-old neighbor when I was only 10. While this sort of exposure is regrettably common for those between the ages of 9 and 12, the experience hit me very deeply. I remember looking at those images as a young boy with a deep sense of intrigue, an innocent curiosity combined with an innate awareness that viewing that stuff didn't seem quite right.

For the next few years following that initial exposure, my curiosity was heightened and a deepening sense of secrecy began to materialize in my life. Long before entering middle school, I was very aware that porn was not something "church kids" were supposed to entertain. And while I was too fearful to stockpile any of my own nudie pictures or magazines (mostly afraid of getting caught), I was enticed by almost any opportunity to lay my eyes on photos of exposed female flesh.

When you add to that the fact that some of my friends (the ones who had satellite dishes the size of flying saucers in their backyards) had access to X-rated material on television, it is no wonder I began receiving quite an education without my parents ever knowing it. Living in a world where young middle school guys regularly viewed this stuff, some of my initial shame was alleviated by the rationalization that "everyone" was doing it.

One innocent afternoon just before turning 15, I came home from school to be greeted with a cassette tape my mom said she wanted me to listen to. I asked her what it was about, and she explained that it was an interview with a guy explaining what can happen to people who look at pornography.

Being that I had never really spoken with my mom about porn, I was awkwardly taken aback by her gesture. Immediately I wondered, "Is she on to me? Does she suspect something? Did I accidentally leave the Sears catalog open to the lingerie section?" I couldn't figure it out, but I agreed I would take a listen.

Later that day, I found some alone time in my room to play the tape. What I was about to hear over the next 30 minutes would almost literally scare me to death. The tape was an interview by Dr. James Dobson – the well-known Evangelical family advice guru and founder of the ministry *Focus on the Family*. His interviewee? Convicted serial killer Ted Bundy, who was awaiting the death penalty for multiple crimes against women of the most gruesome kind.

Bundy had claimed to have received Christ as his Savior while in prison awaiting execution. As Dr. Dobson interviewed the infamous criminal, he asked Bundy to describe how it was possible that a man with a relatively normal upbringing could morph into the heartless monster he had become. Bundy's response? It all began when he started experimenting with pornography as a young man. The moment I heard that testimony was the moment that shame went from merely pushing me around to sinking its teeth deep into my young soul.

I would eventually come to understand that it was never my mother's intention to scar me for life with that interview – but immediately following that episode I began to spiral downward into an abyss of shame and fear that I can only describe as horrifying. Because I did not at that point feel I had a safe adult in my life with which to process my pre-adolescent questions and early sexual exploration, my sexuality became shameful and dirty to me.

As crazy as it may sound, I began to struggle with frequent thoughts of suicide. Horrified by the possibility that I too could become someone like Ted Bundy, my adolescent fears led me to rationalize that I would be better off dead than to hurt someone else so horrifically. This cycle of sin, isolation, fear and anxiety led me to believe that I was the scum of the earth.

By the standards as I now understand them, my teenage sexual curiosities were by no means abnormal. I *had* viewed pornography off and on since that original exposure. I *had* experienced some kissing and mild fondling of girls during those silly middle-school times of "going steady". I *had* developed an affinity for masturbation as most boys do. And while those behaviors are nowhere to be found in the Bible under "Rules for Holy Living", they were certainly not abnormally devious behaviors for an adolescent male.

But like so many other young pre-teens and middle schoolers, I didn't have anyone I felt I could process my sexual development with. I'm not saying that as a twelve year old boy I would have voluntarily gone out looking for coaching in that area, but the point is that no safe adult took the initiative – and shame sunk its teeth in.

Feeling worthless, dirty and struggling with the resulting suicidal ideations I mentioned earlier, my freshman and sophomore years of high school were filled with inner turbulence on top of the "normal" insecurities associated with high school drama. I remember days when I was paralyzed by the fear that I was going to hurt myself or take my own life because I thought I wasn't worth anything. Thankfully, God began to intervene in the nick of time.

Toward the end of my sophomore year – battling the war within and thoroughly frustrated with the notion of God – I was halfway tricked into being a part of a mission team to Mexico with a youth group at a local church in our town. During that trip, God began to awaken me to some realities about His love and passion for the world that began to renew my hope in the possibility that He actually may still love a disgusting individual like me.

It was on that trip that I encountered Jesus in a dramatic way. Shortly thereafter, I began to see my life change significantly in terms of the hope that God may still have a future for me that did not include totally uselessness at best, or suicide at worst.

As I became involved in that youth group, God used my youth pastor in unbelievable ways to help draw me toward the grace and assurance I was craving. In many ways, it was his priceless influence that drew my own heart toward wanting to help other teenagers in the same way God had used him to help me.

For the first time in my life, I began to read the Bible – particularly the New Testament – with relentless fervor. My obsession with mining whatever I could from its pages became so intense that I would arrive home after school to spend literally hours reading Scripture. When my grades began to suffer from my newfound addiction to the Bible, it made for an unusual dilemma for my mom. After all, how in the world does a Christian mother tell her teenage son that he needs to spend *less* time reading his Bible?

My newfound faith was infectious, and during my junior year of high school people across the generational spectrum began to make predictions about my becoming a pastor or Christian leader someday. This dramatic turnaround was in many ways a very affirming reality in my life. I began to believe that perhaps God *did* still love me. Maybe God *did* still have a good plan for my life. But that assurance was put to the test beginning in January of the next year, when I was held hostage in an armed robbery at the local grocery store where I worked during high school.

I obviously lived through that ordeal, and two months later God protected me again through a life-threatening car accident along a busy highway while driving to school one morning. Escaping the wreckage with only minor pain and bruising would not be the last test my faith would endure in that six-month window. A short time later my mother announced to my siblings and I that she would be divorcing our dad – ending an often turbulent marriage of 20 years.

That successive chain of trials – the hostage situation, the car accident, and my parents' divorce – would for the first time since my "spiritual awakening" in Mexico lead me to an experience that I had not yet seriously faced in my budding spiritual journey: *anger with God*. For the previous year, I was under the impression that God and I were now buddies – that all was going to get better – and that my intense shame, bitter doubts and looming questions were finally coming to an end.

Shame and Grace

Having by then developed a reputation as a budding spiritual giant among many of my Christian friends, I tried to respond to those trials exactly how I thought they would expect me to – with confidence and courage. I now had a leadership image to fulfill. I had a game-face to maintain. As a student leader in our youth group who was gaining more and more notoriety for his spiritual maturity, I began to learn how to play the part of a "good Christian".

Ironically, this was the very thing I had grown to despise about many of the Christians I knew during my early years. We were a family who would often fight like crazy all the way to church, only to miraculously emerge from our car as dispensers of plastic smiles and religious jargon like "Hallelujah" and "Praise the Lord, brother..." I am not insinuating that my parents didn't genuinely love God and desire to serve Him. But most kids are very sensitive to what they perceive as hypocrisy. Over time, hypocrisy in the lives of those we are supposed to look up to can be disillusioning.

Pretending to be stronger and more spiritual than I really was became a habit for me. In my late teens I had developed a fairly impressive skill set with regard to duplicity. Because of my Biblical knowledge and communication skills, I could give the appearance of strength to those whom I thought wanted it while continually struggling behind the scenes with anger at God, lack of sexual integrity, and a resurgent sense of shame related to my own hypocrisy.

The season of life immediately after high school was a wilderness of sorts. While I never walked away from God, I definitely drifted spiritually, continuing to play the part of "strong Christian" on Sundays while living my life as close to the edge as I thought I could get away with. Buried beneath the shame and disillusionment, throughout this time God's still small voice kept whispering that He had not given up on me.

In a loving display of fatherly discipline, God used some consequences of my lifestyle to help me re-focus at age 21. I decided that I could no longer be bitter about my family problems, lack of funds for Bible college, etc. Instead, I knew that I had to begin walking by faith again. That's when I moved to southern Oregon, where God graciously renewed my calling into ministry. It was during that time that I met my wife, served on staff at a church for the first time, and eventually moved back to California to enroll at Bible College to begin receiving some formal theological training.

Over the 14 years I served as a youth pastor, God gave my wife and I a fruitful ministry together. And while I am grateful for the ability He gave me to keep His grace front and center toward most of the students He used me to disciple, I explained in the introduction of this book that for years I struggled profoundly with being able to receive and *rest* in that grace for myself.

Shame had for so long been embedded in my psyche that it took many years to experience significant healing and freedom from that bondage. My story is not unique. Compared to the horrifying shame stories of some, my experiences seem like practically nothing. But that is what shame does. That is why it is so diabolical. It will seek to destroy an otherwise healthy individual with the neurotic entanglement of the deepest forms of self-deprecation, self-loathing, insecurity and isolation. There is only one source of power to defeat it, and that power is the uncut gospel of grace.

This is – perhaps more than any other reason – why I am so personally passionate about articulating, preaching and defending the uncut gospel of God's free grace in its purest possible form. Having been told for so many years that a "true" Christian will somehow automatically begin to live in gradual, increasing victory over sin, selfishness and shame, I have finally begun to comprehend that this was the bill of goods I was being sold by the back-loaders. I was told that if I would only study my Bible more, pray more, share my faith more and serve God more – if I would "simply" be holy as God is holy (whatever that meant) – that the "feelings" of assurance would come later.

Well, they didn't come. For years, they didn't come. No matter how fervently I preached grace and believed in eternal security and pleaded for God's power in my life, the peace never arrived…at least not for long. There was always the occasional spiritual "high" after a great event. But within hours or days, I was right back onto the performance treadmill, working and sweating and toiling while going absolutely nowhere. Until…

Until I began to understand the difference between *resting* and *wrestling*. Grace calls us to a life of *rest*. In pointing us toward the New Covenant ministry He was about to institute, Jesus Christ invited us with the wonderful offer I will repeat yet again:

> Grace calls us to a life of *rest*.

> Come to me, all you who are weary and burdened, and I will
> give you rest. Take my yoke upon you and learn from me, for
> I am gentle and humble in heart, and *you will find rest* for your
> souls. For my yoke is easy and my burden is light.[63]

Notice what Jesus says will happen when we come to Him for rest: we *will find* it. When I finally began to take those words seriously – combined with the fact that I was *not* consistently experiencing anything that felt even remotely like "rest" in my journey with God – I began to realize that it was time to get painfully honest. Either Jesus was a total liar, or I was not really coming to Him for rest.

I say it was time to get "painfully honest" because that's exactly what it feels like to a person who has preached a message of grace for so long without ever really consistently experiencing its benefits in practical ways. Oh sure, I knew I was saved. I knew by faith that what I was teaching was true. But the same grace that had saved me was somehow not translating into *daily* peace of mind and heart.

On the rare occasion that I would actually open up to someone about my struggles with shame, I was usually told that I was experiencing spiritual warfare. And for the record, I do not disagree with this assessment. I believe in spiritual warfare as an unquestionable reality in the life of a believer in Christ. What I did not understand was the difference between *resting* and *wrestling*. Most teaching on spiritual warfare is focused on "wrestling." But in the pages of the New Testament, I discovered a different path. More about that in the next chapter...

Chapter 10: Relaxing on the Battle Field

As a believer in and proclaimer of the uncut gospel of grace, I understand there is a reality we Christians commonly refer to as "spiritual warfare." We rightly base these beliefs on various Biblical teachings related to the activities of Satan and his demons attempting to disrupt or diminish the plans, purposes and people of God.

I was taught – as were many Christians – that whenever I felt like I was under spiritual attack, it was my duty to either "bind" or "rebuke" the devil. In other words, I was rightly taught that because of my position as a believer in Christ, I had authority over the demonic realm.

Based on this authority I was taught that whenever spiritual attacks came (usually in the form of temptation, doubt, fear, etc.) I should speak to those spiritual forces of evil with phrases such as "Satan, I bind you (or rebuke you) in the name of Jesus." I was taught that in doing this, the devil and his demons were required to leave me alone.

Perhaps you have been led to believe and practice something similar by well-intentioned spiritual leaders. After all, Jesus spoke to Satan by quoting verses from Deuteronomy when he was being tempted (Matt. 4; Luke 4). If Jesus is our ultimate example, perhaps we also should follow him by affirming Scriptural truths to the devil whenever he attacks us…right?

It sounded reasonable, but the more I began to grow in my understanding of God's power, the finished work of Jesus and my union with Him through faith, the more I began to see that speaking directly to Satan is not something Paul or the other New Testament writers instructed us to do. While it is certainly true that Jesus is our supreme example, I have been drilling home the point that we need to be careful to understand many of the actions that Christ took in their proper historic and theological context.

When Jesus spoke to Satan in Matthew 4 and Luke 4, I do not believe that he was necessarily giving His future New Covenant disciples a model for how to walk in victory over the ploys of the devil. As I have repeatedly affirmed, we must not forget that the majority of Jesus' earthly ministry occurred *prior* to His death and resurrection. The provisions that He made for us by going to the cross were not yet in full effect in the Matthew 4 and Luke 4 accounts. That reality *has* to be considered as we interpret such passages.

When Jesus went to the cross, the composite witness of the New Testament writings affirm that something drastic occurred.[64] The Epistles repeatedly teach us that Satan's impact was dramatically undercut, rendering him powerless to do virtually anything other than to spread lies and deception.

I remember once seeing a slogan on a T-shirt at a Christian festival that boasted *"The next time the devil reminds you of your past, remind him of his future."* While the point may sound reasonable enough, in reality the best way to overcome the work of Satan is *not* to engage in conversation with Him at all, but to simply *rest* in the finished work of Jesus Christ on our behalf!

Fighting *For* or Fighting *From*?

When Jesus rose from the dead, he declared victory over death and the prince of death – Satan himself. The New Testament teaches that when we become children of God through belief in Christ's saving work, we become "joint-heirs" with Him concerning all the spiritual blessings of God. This literally means that we are placed in union *with Christ* in His victory over Satan (Rom. 8:17; Eph. 3:6; Gal. 3:29).

As Christians, we are never to fight for a position of victory over Satan. Instead, we are to fight *from* a position of victory that is already ours, realizing by faith that God has already defeated him and that we don't need to entertain his lies and intimidations.

Additionally, not only is the idea of a Christian "binding" Satan totally absent from Scripture, but it is also very illogical to pray to an angel. That is, after all, what Satan is – a fallen angel!

Think about it. You don't wake up in the morning and pray "Dear Gabriel…or Dear Michael the Archangel…I ask for this or that…." That would be ridiculous! Instead, you address your Heavenly Father directly.

We are not to pray to angels – whether they be holy angels or fallen angels! We pray to God alone and then *rest* in the assurance that *He* will command His angels if necessary to protect us and that *He* will defend us against the attacks of Satan by all necessary means.

Can the Devil Get Me?

A very common question I have received as a pastor is "what about demon-possession?" Does it exist today? I believe it does exist. There is nothing I can find in the Scriptures to indicate that demon possession has ceased now that the New Covenant era has begun. The book of Acts – which was written *after* Christ's death and resurrection detailing His early New Covenant ministry – highlights a few examples of people being possessed by demonic spirits (ex. Acts 8:7; 16:18).

I do not however, accept the notion that believers in Jesus can be demon-possessed. When a person becomes a child of God through faith in Jesus, God places that person "in Christ." While Christians can certainly open themselves up to Satan's influence and deception by willfully walking in disobedience to God, they cannot be "possessed" by demons, since possession denotes *ownership*.

A person's soul cannot have two owners. When Jesus Christ saves a person – He permanently "seals" that person with His Holy Spirit, and that seal cannot be broken (Eph. 1:13). No matter what, Satan can *never* have a person back who has been rescued from sin and death through Christ![65]

Yet another question I have been asked is equally important: "Can Satan or his demons 'read' our thoughts?" The answer is no. Nowhere does New Testament Scripture indicate that these spiritual entities can read our thoughts. Fallen angels are not omniscient beings. What they *can* apparently do is understand our weaknesses and the fallen tendencies of our flesh.

This means that Satan and his forces can anticipate where we are most likely to fall – and they are able to place landmines in our path in order to trap or tempt us. They do this using lies and deception, because their real power has been stripped through Christ's triumph on the cross.

This is why sin among believers is not always the result of blatant acts of rebellion, but of the less obvious result of forgetting who we really are in Christ. Satan and his forces will lure our flesh into looking somewhere *other than Christ* for fulfillment, and that is where a lot of our sinful behavior comes from.

If Jesus Won the War, How Do We Win the Battles?

Finally, these realities bring us to what is perhaps the most important question for those who understand the security of their position in grace. If we are not commanded to *bind* or *rebuke* the devil as is the practice of so many, and if Satan is essentially limited to the weapons of lies and deception, then how *should* we relate to our spiritual enemy? What does it mean to "resist him" and "take our stand" against him as we are taught in the New Testament (James 4:7; 1 Pet. 5:9)? Fortunately, the Apostle Paul left Christ's church with an indispensible guide in Ephesians 6.

When we come to a point of understanding *who* our enemy is – combined with a realistic picture of his strengths and weaknesses – we can operate in a way that honors the uncut gospel and brings positive results to the world (and to our personal lives as well). As we work through Ephesians 6:10-18 in the pages that follow, we are going to discover *five core truths* that will greatly assist us in our dealings with our spiritual adversary, Satan. Paul writes this indispensible passage as follows...

> Finally, be strong in the Lord and in his mighty power. Put on the full armor of God so that you can take your stand against the devil's schemes. For our struggle is not against flesh and blood, but against the rulers, against the authorities, against the powers of this dark world and against the spiritual forces of evil in the heavenly realms.

> Therefore put on the full armor of God, so that when the day of evil comes, you may be able to stand your ground, and after you have done everything, to stand. Stand firm then, with the belt of truth buckled around your waist, with the breastplate of righteousness in place, and with your feet fitted with the readiness that comes from the gospel of peace. In addition to all this, take up the shield of faith, with which you can extinguish all the flaming arrows of the evil one. Take the helmet of salvation and the sword of the Spirit, which is the word of God. And pray in the Spirit on all occasions with all kinds of prayers and requests. With this in mind, be alert and always keep on praying for all the saints.

Truth #1: The Security of our Identity

In Ephesians 6:10, Paul taught believers to "be strong *in the Lord and in his mighty power*" (italics mine). The phrase "in the Lord" is the key operative term for not only this passage, but for the entire book of Ephesians and much of Paul's teaching elsewhere. Our position of being "in Christ" or "in Him" or "in the Lord" or "in the Spirit" is repeated over and over throughout the message of Ephesians, particularly in the first chapter.

When Paul begins to close out the letter with his thoughts on spiritual warfare, he is using this phrase "in the Lord" to emphasize everything he has already said about the new identity we have been given through faith alone in Christ alone. Remember, we are not to fight *for* a position of spiritual victory. Rather, we are to fight *from* a position of the victory which has already been handed to us in Christ as a free gift purchased by His blood. Paul is reminding believers of this.

Hence, we are called to *rest* in the security of our *identity*. We are now *in the Lord* – united with Him in spirit and indwelled by His unquenchable presence. Battling Satan is not to be a white-knuckled, fearful endeavor full of stress or intimidation. Because of what Christ has irreversibly accomplished, we are strong and secure "in the Lord."

Truth #2: *The Reality of the Invasion*

It is a general truism that perhaps the only thing *worse* than giving Satan more credit than he deserves is when we fail to believe in the reality of his schemes. There is an old Keith Green song from the late 1970's called *No One Believes in Me Anymore*. The song identifies this as Satan's boast. One of the lyrics in the song says, from the viewpoint of Satan,*"I used to have to sneak around, but now they just open their door. No one's watching for my tricks, 'cause no one believes in me anymore."*

Those lyrics are true – that people are sometimes oblivious to the reality of Satan's work even though the Bible teaches repeatedly that Satan *is* real and that his stubborn schemes to disrupt, distort and destroy the plan of God are also real. The Apostle Paul writes in verses 11-12:

> Put on the full armor of God so that you can take your stand against the devil's schemes. For our struggle is not against flesh and blood, but against the rulers, against the authorities, against the powers of this dark world and against the spiritual forces of evil in the heavenly realms.

Based on these words alone, there can be no doubt that the Bible affirms we are in a battle with "spiritual forces of evil in the heavenly realms." There has been an invasion of dark angelic forces upon planet earth. And because these forces are masters of deception led by the master deceiver himself, they have successfully coerced billions of people to cooperate with their schemes.

Paul says we are to take our stand "against the devil's schemes" and he says we are to do this by "putting on the full armor of God..." To rest in grace does not mean to deny the existence of Satan's schemes or to minimize His power to deceive. But it does mean that we do not fight spiritual battles with tactics that Paul elsewhere describes as "carnal" or of the flesh.[66]

Instead, we are to go to battle armed with the all-sufficient work of Jesus in our favor. He already fought the ultimate battle and won it through the cross and empty tomb, having disarmed Satan's powers. By His grace, he has passed that victory on to us because we are now identified "with him".[67]

By grace, the spiritual victory belonging to Jesus also belongs to us. Satan's only debilitating weapon is to deceive us into believing otherwise so that we will struggle with the neurotic insecurities associated with failing to rest in His finished work.

> By grace, the spiritual victory belonging to Jesus also belongs to us.

Truth #3: The Simplicity of the Instructions

Ephesians 6:13 continues, "Therefore put on the full armor of God, so that when the day of evil comes, you may be able to stand your ground, and after you have done everything, to stand."

Paul's instructions about spiritual battle are not complicated. He never gives us an elaborate, conspiratorial plan to "map out" demonic territories around our neighborhoods and cities. He makes no mention of believers organizing militant prayer-walks in order to be sure we will take Satan down. He simply says – for a second time – "put on the full armor of God", so that when the day of evil comes we will be able to stand strong. The instructions are definitely simple!

Let me ask you a very practical question: "Is your spiritual journey one which can be characterized as *restful*? Is your life full of peace and assurance?" I'm not asking whether you experience any pain, chaos or confusion. We all do as a by-product of living in a fallen world. What I'm asking is: "In the midst of *whatever* is going on in your life at any given moment – is your spiritual journey a joyous one? Or is it typically filled with fear, anxiety and confusion?"

Have you taken Jesus up on His offer to *come and experience His rest* or are you white-knuckling your way through life's battles, paranoid about what's around the corner? That's not what it means to engage in spiritual warfare. That's the neurotic effect of bad religious teaching!

You are *more* than a conqueror in Christ! That is how God's Word defines you beginning the moment you place your childlike trust in Christ![68] This isn't a psychological exercise in the power of positive thinking! This is simply taking God at His Word – which, by the way, is bound to have a positive impact on your psyche as well! So what exactly does it *mean* to put on this armor of God? Paul tells us...

Truth #4: The Availability of the Inventory

Once we realize that we are to "put on" the armor, we need to understand what that armor actually consists of so that we can apply it to our lives! Thankfully, Paul gives us a succinct inventory of the armor God provides through the finished work of Christ. Let's take another look at the wardrobe he describes and then we will consider each piece individually...

> Stand firm then, with the *belt of truth* buckled around your waist, with the *breastplate of righteousness* in place, and with your *feet fitted* with the readiness that comes from the gospel of peace. In addition to all this, take up the *shield of faith*, with which you can extinguish all the flaming arrows of the evil one. Take the *helmet of salvation* and the *sword of the Spirit*, which is the word of God. (vv. 14-17)

The Belt

In this passage, the first piece of armor Paul mentions is what he calls *the belt of truth*. This piece is rightly mentioned first because – as we've already noted – Satan's only real remaining weapons are lies and deception. Some of his strategic head-games include, but are not limited to...

- intimidating us
- making us believe he is stronger than he actually is
- getting us to believe he doesn't actually exist
- convincing us that his plan is more attractive than God's
- making us believe that there loopholes in the sufficiency of God's grace for us
- telling us there is more we must add to Christ's finished work
- leading us to question the legitimacy of our new life, nature and identity in Christ

He operates in all sorts of deceptive ways, and we are called to overcome his lies with the truth. Again, this fact is saturated with the necessity of understanding the truth about what Jesus accomplished for us through the cross and resurrection.

It is significant to note that the belt was actually the fundamental piece of armor in the ancient world. Roman citizens wore robes and would gird them in their belts in order to move into battle in a less restricted manner. Additionally, the sword hung from the belt, and the breastplate was also connected to it.

At this point we might naturally ask the question "What *is* the truth about what Christ accomplished for us on the cross?" Among other places, Colossians and Hebrews describe the answer as follows:

> "He forgave us all our sins, having canceled the written code (the Law), with its regulations, that was against us and that stood opposed to us; He took it away, nailing it to the cross. And *having disarmed the powers and authorities, he made a public spectacle of them, triumphing over them by the cross.*" (Colossians 2:13-15)

"Since the children (of God) have flesh and blood, he too shared in their humanity so that *by his death he might destroy him who holds the power of death – that is, the devil –* and free those who all their lives were held in slavery by their fear of death." (Hebrews 2:14)

And of course, there is that glorious moment on the cross when Jesus cries out, "It is finished!" signifying that His defeat of Satan and redemption of sinners was in full effect for anyone who would receive that gracious gift by faith![69] If we are going to rest in grace as followers of Jesus, we need to make a decision: Do we *believe* God or not? *Has* Satan been defeated or not? The truth is that he *has* indeed been defeated at the cross, and we are to wear that truth as the central piece of armor like a belt around our waist!

> If we are going to rest in grace as followers of Jesus, we need to make a decision: Do we *believe* God or not? *Has* Satan been defeated or not?

The Breastplate

Secondly, Paul mentions that we are to have "the breastplate of righteousness in place." We have to keep in mind that as Paul is writing this he is under house arrest and subject to round-the-clock surveillance by the Roman guards. Undoubtedly, the Holy Spirit is giving Paul this revelation about spiritual "armor" as he is looking at the very equipment worn by those guards who would change shifts every few hours to keep watch over him. In view of this armor, he brings up the "breastplate of righteousness".

As Paul looked at the breastplate on the guards responsible for his oversight, he would have known that this piece of armor was created to guard the heart and other vital organs. The breastplate of righteousness is exactly what God gives us to guard our spiritual vitality as well.

When we place our faith in Christ, the provisions of the cross are applied to our lives – permanently removing the record of our past, present and future acts of sin. Not only is the debt of our sin canceled, but a *positive* transaction also occurs as God "gives us" the righteous perfection of Jesus Christ in the place of our former unrighteousness. In essence, our Heavenly Judge "rules in our favor" and declares that we are no longer guilty as sinners even though we deserved the full penalty for our sins. This new life of innocence and righteousness is both positional and *actual* upon receiving Christ.

> God made him who had no sin to be sin for us, so that in him we might become the righteousness of God. (2 Corinthians 5:21).

The battle really begins to rage when Satan uses his lies – and even our own mistakes and sins – against us to make us feel insecure before God. Satan is elsewhere described as our "accuser" (Rev. 12:10) and he attempts to impugn us day and night before the Judge of the universe. *That* is when the breastplate of righteousness begins to do its most significant work, as we choose to rest in the irreversible fact of our righteous new standing and nature in Christ!

Even when we willfully sin – while there may be earthly consequences in the wake of our rebellion – God's disposition of tenderness and grace toward us remains untainted and undeterred. If you are a child of God by grace through faith in Christ – you have the breastplate of righteousness to guard your soul against Satan's accusations. Think about this wonderful reality! If the only Being in the entire universe who has the power and right to condemn you has decided not to, then who are you to condemn yourself, much less allow Satan to do such a thing with his lies?

> Even when we willfully sin – while there may be earthly consequences in the wake of our rebellion – God's disposition of tenderness and grace toward us remains untainted and undeterred.

The Footwear

Thirdly, Paul identifies this issue of our feet being "fitted with the readiness that comes from the gospel of peace." Paul knew that when a soldier went to battle, he or she needed reliable footwear! And he identifies the "gospel of peace" as that armor that will keep our feet from slipping.

The uncut gospel of grace is also rightly referred to as the gospel of peace, for it brings God's peace into our lives. If you are a believer in Jesus, you are at peace *with* God. No longer are you at odds with God because the debt produced by your sin has been fully paid for. Since you are now at peace *with* God by grace through faith, you have the opportunity to experience the peace *of* God as one of the pre-eminent qualities of your daily life.

Peace *with* God is objective, based on God's cleansing from sin and impartation of new life to our spirit. The peace *of* God is subjective, to be experienced in greater consistency as a we consciously rest in Him.

Earlier in Ephesians, Paul states that Jesus himself "is our peace". He has broken down the dividing wall between God and us – and also between Jews and Gentiles.[70] He has demolished the power of anything that would stand between us experiencing peace of heart and mind in our relationships with self and others.

When we are not at peace, the first thing we need to ask is "what *lies* are we believing?" Think about that for a moment. When I am in a relational struggle, what are some of the lies I could be believing? I could be believing that...

- If I could only *control* that other person, I would be happy!
- If I could only make them *accept* my viewpoint, I would be happy!
- If I could only get *revenge*, I would be happy!

On and on goes the list of lies! The truth is that there is only *one* thing that is going to make us happy, and that is realizing and resting in the fact that we are infinitely, irrationally and irreversibly *loved* and *accepted* by our Creator. When we are at rest in that reality, we can more easily let go of those other control issues that tend to bring such a *lack* of peace into our human relationships.

The Shield

Fourthly, there is the "shield of faith". This shield, we are told, is what will extinguish all the "flaming arrows of the evil one." A lot of bad religious teaching has served to hijack the meaning of simple faith. Faith is not a force of power that we conjure up within ourselves in order to make God do what we want – as certain televangelists have been known to claim – but rather it is a disposition of complete *trust* in God.

> Faith is not a force of power that we conjure up within ourselves in order to make God do what we want ...
>
> ... but rather it is a disposition of complete *trust* in God.

According to Hebrews, faith is "being sure of what we hope for and certain of what we do not yet see" (Heb. 11:1). It is the personal confidence that something God has said or done on your behalf is true.

In the heat of battle, it is common for us to take our eyes off the ball. Like Peter walking on the water in the midst of the storm, it is easy to turn our gaze *away* from the beauty and reality of Jesus and instead allow the thrashing waves to freak us out! Faith is what keeps us calm in the midst of the battle – in the midst of whatever comes our way.

Faith is not a denial of reality. Rather, it is the assurance that God is still on His throne and working in our best interests even when reality is difficult or painful! Paul uses this analogy of the shield to illustrate that piece of armor which protects us when the battle is at its fiercest point.

Faith is the example we see in Jesus crying out in the Garden of Gethsemane in the moments before His arrest and trial, "Abba, if there be any way, please take this cup of suffering from me! Yet, not my will, but Yours be done!"[71] If you and I can learn to rest so completely in Christ that we experience *that* level of comfort before God, there is *nothing* that can bring us down in this life! Absolutely *nothing*! And we *can* learn to live this way. God's indwelling Spirit guarantees it!

The Helmet

Fifthly, Paul mentions the helmet of salvation. Most likely, Paul is using the term salvation here in the same sense he used it in 1 Thessalonians 5:8 when he told them to put on "the hope of salvation as a helmet." In the context of that passage, he is referring to the promised "deliverance" or "rescue" that Jesus will bring when He returns for His Church in the future.

The helmet protects the head, which is the control center of the body. The helmet of salvation essentially reminds us that the difficulties we experience in this life are as *close to hell* as we will ever have to get – and that even in the midst of hell on earth, tastes and glimpses of heaven are our to enjoy!

The helmet of salvation secures us in the perspective that our brothers and sisters across the centuries have lived by – that this world as we *currently* know it is not our home nor our ultimate destiny! The helmet of salvation reminds us that as we allow God's peace and justice to flow through *our* lives on this earth, the fullness of the kingdom will ultimately come when the King of kings and Lord of lords establishes His heaven-on-earthly reign in the future that awaits us![72]

As American Christians, our perspective on this reality can be easily diminished by comparison to many other Christians in the world. We live in a society that has long been attempting to create "heaven on earth" – a culture that is grasping for a utopian state of existence because secular humanism has coerced people to believe that this temporal life is all there is!

Because of our affluent way of life and the many distractions competing for our attention, too few of us *long* for Christ's return in the same way that many of our brothers and sisters long for it around the globe. My hope is that the more God's children grow in grace, the more we will be longing again for the return of Jesus Christ, and allowing the Spirit to live through us in demonstrating grace and truth toward friends and enemies alike. This is the helmet of salvation – living in the joyous anticipation that our Deliverer is coming (and perhaps soon!).

> My hope is that the more God's children grow in grace, the more we will be longing again for the return of Jesus Christ, and allowing the Spirit to live through us in demonstrating grace and truth toward friends and enemies alike.

The Sword

Finally, after Paul identifies *five* defensive weapons, he concludes with mention of a single offensive weapon: the "sword of the Spirit, which is the Word of God." The Word of God has been manifest to humanity in two primary ways:

1) The Living Word – Jesus who came in the flesh to rescue us, and...
2) The Written Word – the Old and New Testament Scriptures

Bible-believing followers of Jesus are commonly labeled as *Evangelical* Christians. If you can get past the expanding cultural stigma which increasingly equates the word "Evangelical" with "fundamentalist bigot", perhaps you can appreciate how amazing that label really is!

To be *Evangelical* is to be committed to the proclamation and demonstration of the uncut gospel of grace revealed in the Scriptures. It refers to a passion for reaching people with the message that Jesus Christ is the ultimate *point* of the whole universe, that He has come to redeem His fallen creation, and that He offers a relationship with God to *whosoever* believes in Him! If you really want to know how to rise above the kingdom of darkness in your life, ask God to help you become more passionate about the advance of the uncut gospel throughout every tribe, tongue and nation of the earth!

In the most *clearly* stated reason in the Bible as to why Jesus has not returned to earth yet, 2 Peter 3:9 says that it is because God is "patient" with humanity, not wanting anyone to perish, but for *everyone* to come to repentance.

Isn't it amazing to think that God would hold back His judgment and the final implementation of His kingdom long enough for as many people as possible to receive Christ as their Savior? When we become excited about trusting the Word of God fully and advancing the gospel it reveals, we then become truly *dangerous* to the forces of darkness!

Lastly, after teaching us about the security of our identity, the reality of the invasion, the simplicity of the instructions, and the availability of the inventory, Paul finishes his thoughts by focusing on a fifth and final reality...

Truth #5: The Opportunity for Intercession

Paul concludes his words on spiritual warfare in Ephesians 6:18, exhorting the believers to "pray in the Spirit on all occasions with all kinds of prayers and requests. With this in mind, be alert and always keep on praying for all the saints."

He closes out his exhortation with a plea for them to be immersed in prayer. How often? On all occasions! What kind of prayer? All kinds of prayer! More than anything else, prayer is simply communing with God – bringing our requests, longings, frustrations, questions, doubts, fears and praises to Him with bold confidence.

The one who rests in grace finds prayer an increasing delight – not a legalistic regimen or so-called "spiritual discipline" by which to fulfill a perceived duty. There is no "proper" time and place to pray – any more than there is a "proper" regimen for communicating with your spouse or children or parents or close friends. The prayers of those who approach God from a position of rest rather than religious duty are windows offering the experience of boundless intimacy with the God who loved us so much that He would rather die than live without us!

It is at this point that we can begin to discover and live with confidence the life that God has called each of us to experience individually and corporately as His Church. Satan may be our accuser – but Jesus Christ is our *Advocate*. The witness of the Advocate is much brighter and more powerful than the charges of the accuser! The Bible suggests in Revelation that believers ultimately overcome Satan by two major realities: 1) the blood of the Lamb, which stands in our defense against the accuser and forever preserves our righteousness in Christ and 2) by the word of our testimony (Rev. 12:10).

> The prayers of those who approach God from a position of rest rather than religious duty are windows offering the experience of boundless intimacy with the God who loved us so much that He would rather die than live without us!

As believers in the uncut gospel of grace, we tend to place a lot of emphasis on the blood of the Lamb, and rightly so. However, we may have more to discover about the power of our testimony. The truth is that every child of God on planet earth has a testimony. And while our stories differ widely in precise detail, there are many threads of commonality that unify us in the journey toward discovering the truth found in Christ. These include that God has…

- transferred us from darkness to light (Col. 1:13)
- crucified our old man with Himself and made us completely new (Gal. 2:20; 2 Cor. 5:21)
- made us into new creations - the old is gone, the new is come (2 Cor. 5:17)
- placed us "in Christ" as our new identity (Eph. 1:1-11)
- sealed us with His Holy Spirit (Eph. 1:12-13)
- irreversibly secured us in our salvation (1 Pet. 1:3-9)
- offered us freedom from the domination of sin (Rom. 6:1-14)
- given us mercies that are new every morning (Lam. 3:23)
- worked all things out for our good (Rom. 8:28)

-   and offered us grace in which we rest assured of His all-sufficiency (Heb. 4:16)

As children of God, we have been purchased with the blood of Christ. Satan and his demons do not have any ownership or real power over us! We are completely loved, totally secure and irreversibly forgiven by the only One who ever had the right to judge us in the first place! Freedom is now our birthright (Galatians 5:1). We are free from the control of Satan's dominion, and we have the power to begin resting in the freedom that is already ours!

Don't *ever* let the accusations of the enemy convince you that you have fallen beyond the grip of God's grace! You have the blood of the Lamb and the word of your testimony – both of which speak to the fact that you are a brand new creature in Christ, regardless of whatever hurts, habits or hang-

> Don't *ever* let the accusations of the enemy convince you that you have fallen beyond the grip of God's grace!

ups you currently struggle with. The truth *will* set you free, and in the next chapter we will find out how.

Chapter 11: New Covenant Disciples (Grace to Obey)

I can almost hear the voices now: "I knew it! I *knew* that eventually you would get around to the very thing you've been confronting in this book by tacking on a late chapter about obeying the rules! After all this time you've spent promoting the no-strings-attached gospel of grace-through-faith apart from any additional requirements, now you're going to include your own version of the "fine print," focusing on everything God *expects* of us after we receive His supposedly *free gift*!"

The truth is I am about to do no such thing. In fact, my prayer is that by the end of this book, you will begin to see obedience to Christ from a perspective that will revolutionize your spiritual journey from this day forward!

I realize that the bait-and-switch approach is what you are accustomed to hearing and reading about in so much of popular Christian literature. As a cursory example of this, consider the following statements from a few popular voices...

> But if "good works" (activities of serving God and others) do not follow from our profession of faith, we are as yet believing

only from the head, not from the heart: in other words, justifying faith…is not yet ours.[73] (emphasis mine).

Did you catch that? Here is a leading Evangelical theologian
making the false differentiation between so-called "head faith" and
"heart faith" or between "justifying (saving) faith" and "non-justifying
(non-saving) faith" when the Bible makes no such distinction! As we
discussed in chapter 4, the Word of God is concerned with the *object*
of our faith and not a superficial dualistic argument we've created over
"head versus heart". Consider another example…

> Scripture puts repentance and faith together as different
> aspects of the one act of coming to Christ for salvation. It is
> not that a person first turns from sin and next trusts in Christ,
> or first trusts in Christ and then turns from sin, but rather that
> both occur at the same time.[74]

Notice how this statement deviates from the uncut gospel of grace.
Of course, if we define repentance accurately as "a change of mind"
from unbelief to belief, then there is no problem linking repentance
to faith as one synonymous act – and therefore, the sole condition of
salvation.

However, the statement above clearly views repentance as a
"turning from sin" – and demands that this disposition is a necessary
part of true "saving" faith. Again, this goes beyond the scope of the
Biblical meaning of simple faith in Jesus.

If you'll remember, the thief on the cross had no opportunity
to "turn from his sin" when he cried out to Jesus, "Remember me
when you enter your Father's Kingdom." He didn't try to cut a deal by
promising he would change his ways if only Jesus would rescue Him.
He simply realized his need for a Savior, and that Jesus *was* that Savior.
His simple act of trust (faith) was enough to receive the gift of entering
paradise with the Father and the Son.[75] And in reference to the James
2 passage we considered in chapter 4, one commentator writes

James now offers a rational argument in order to show that while there may be a type of "faith" that does not issue forth in deeds, such faith is dead; *it has no saving power*. True faith, he insists, always changes the heart and therefore results in acts of mercy and compassion."[76] (emphasis mine).

Based upon the above description of so-called saving faith, one would think that if a professing believer were somehow to demonstrate anything *less* than a life chalk full of amazing sacrificial deeds, he or she would have no real reason to rest assured they were saved. As we have stated previously, herein lies a fundamental problem with Lordship Salvation. With that in mind, I offer one more example:

> The thought of a person calling himself a "Christian" without being a devoted follower of Jesus is absurd....So we can follow our own course while still calling ourselves followers of Christ? So we can join the Marines, so to speak, without having to do all the work?[77]

That last statement is one of the most egregious misrepresentations of the gospel I have heard in quite some time. Suggesting that being a Christian and joining the Marines are even remotely analogous is too consequential to ignore.

Let me be clear that I am only addressing the statement, and not condemning the author himself. I have zero doubt that the gifted author who wrote this wants essentially the same thing as I want: for the Body of Christ to grow in love, holiness and global impact. However, we apparently disagree on how to get there.

For one thing, the U.S. Marines are some of the most well-trained warriors in the world. You don't get into the Marines without passing a number of stringent tests. And you certainly don't continue in the Marines without proving that you've got what it takes. These are wonderful and necessary requirements for building a body of warriors to defend a nation, but they are far from reflective of the requirements for inclusion in God's kingdom.

The Apostle Paul offers quite a contrast to this Marine-Corps analogy when he talks about Christ's recruitment process. He says

> Brothers, think of what you were when you were called. *Not many of you were wise by human standards; not many were influential; not many were of noble birth.* But *God chose the foolish things of the world* to shame the wise; *God chose the weak things* of the world to shame the strong. *He chose the lowly things* of this world *and the despised things*—and *the things that are not*—to nullify the things that are, so that no one may boast before him. It is *because of him* that you are in Christ Jesus, *who has become for us wisdom from God—that is, our righteousness, holiness and redemption.* Therefore, as it is written: "Let him who boasts boast in the Lord."[78] (emphasis mine).

Those standards are not exactly a script for a U.S. Military recruiting tool! The Marines don't take losers. They don't have much tolerance for fools or weaklings. But apparently God does! And throughout history He has found glory in choosing and using some of the world's most unlikely misfits to accomplish His greatest purposes. The stories of these men and women glare at us from the pages of Scripture with an almost embarrassing level of honesty.

To put it bluntly, the heroes of the Bible are usually not from the top tier of the moral gene-pool. They are people who struggled with murder, adultery, dishonesty, fear, doubt, anxiety, unfaithfulness, depression, anger, and oftentimes a lack of "surrender" so severe that calling them our heroes almost borders on insanity. If surrender to Christ's Lordship were a rigid requirement for salvation – much less service to the Lord – God's plan would have failed from the very onset.

Essentially, LS raises the unanswerably subjective question: *"How surrendered to Christ's Lordship must a person be in order to experience assurance of salvation?"* How can we objectively determine who's in and who's out if our criteria rests upon the *performance* of the servant rather than upon the *promises* of the Savior? And yet the crucial question still remains: *What about obedience? What about "living our lives for Jesus"? Doesn't God want to change our lives?*

Well, no…not exactly.

He wants much *more* than that!

Religion can *easily* change a person's life. Getting married or having a baby can change a person's life. Winning the lottery can change a person's life. Heck, an ingrown toenail can change a person's life! At the core, the practical power of the uncut gospel is about much more than a *changed life*. It's about an *exchange life*.

Two Natures or One?

The theological concept of a dual nature is as impractical as it is unbiblical. When Paul speaks of the gospel, he speaks in terms of a death having taken place. He says that as a believer in Christ he has been crucified with Him and no longer lives (Galatians 2:20). He says that the "old self" of every believer has been crucified with Jesus (Romans 6:6).

These realities are spoken of using grammatical constructs that affirm past, completed action. As we established earlier in this book, never in the New Covenant epistles are believers commanded to live by a "die-to-self" mentality of discipleship. We have *already* been crucified with Him – and raised to life with Him as partakers in the power of His resurrection both now and for eternity!

The Bible teaches clearly that when we were born, we were born in the nature of Adam (Genesis 5:3; Romans 1:12-13). The Adamic nature is our "old self" or "old man". At the core of the New Covenant, God promises to *exchange* our hearts of stone for hearts that are soft toward Him and the things He cares about. When we receive Christ as Savior, the spiritual crucifixion of our Adamic nature occurs, and we are given a completely new, righteous nature – the very nature of

Jesus Himself! *He* is now at the root of our identity – not Adam. We are "in Christ" and He is "in us."

The Focus is the Root, Not the Fruit

The overwhelming emphasis of the New Testament with regard to the Christian life is placed not upon the fruit – but rather the root – of the believer's journey. Certainly Jesus wants for His followers to bear fruit (John 15:1-6), but as we affirmed in the previous chapter, everything about the Christian life flows from the reality of being rooted "in Christ".

His substantive life and presence in which we are placed and rooted is the focus of literally *everything* pertaining to the process of sanctification (growing in our practical "set-apartness" as God's children in the world). Apart from being "in Christ" nothing else about sanctification would matter or exist.

If a life-long litany of good works were the key to our assurance of salvation, then millions of cult-members would be falsely secure in their faith. In fact, this is precisely what we see happening in countless man-made religions and pseudo-Christian cults. Religious manipulation combined with strong peer-based community has the power to outwardly reform the behavior of many who then falsely believe that they are accepted by God – at least in part – on the basis of the alleged outward "evidence" of their behavior.

The stunningly glorious truth found in Jesus Christ which sets the gospel uniquely apart from man-made religious claims is that the Savior did not come to make naughty people nice, but to make dead people alive! Man-made religion is primarily focused on making the naughty nice! It's about control and conformity to whatever standard that particular religion demands. But only the uncut gospel of Jesus has the power to make a spiritually dead person live! And yet, this *aliveness* happens – as one might grow to expect from Jesus – in a very unconventional way! Paul gave us the secret to living the Christian life in Galatians 2:20:

> "I have been crucified with Christ and *I no longer live, but Christ lives in me.* The life I live in the body, I live by faith in the Son of God, who loved me and gave himself for me".

Just as Jesus invited his hearers to come and die when He was pointing them toward their need for the cross, Paul now points believers to the finished reality of the cross – affirming that the focus of Christian living is not about dying to ourselves, as so many well-meaning teachers claim. Rather, the focus of Paul's view of sanctification is to accept *by faith* that we have been crucified with Christ – such that we not only *have partaken* in His death, but we are *perpetually partaking* in His resurrection – His life! The phrase "I have been crucified" is in the perfect tense, which Biblical grammarians agree signifies "past completed action with abiding results."[79]

Jesus *Lived* For Me Too!

So many believers rightly emphasize the substitutionary *death* of Christ while seemingly ignoring His equally subtitutionary *life*! We cannot forget that He not only died to pay the just penalty for our sin, but He now *lives* in order that the "the righteous requirements of the law might be met in us who do not live according to the flesh, but according to the Spirit" (Romans 8:4). Not only is His life substitutionary in terms of Him living in perfection prior to the cross, but He now offers to live His life through us on a daily basis as our resurrected Lord and Savior. As Paul wrote so powerfully, we are "saved by his life" (Rom. 5:10).

One of the most well-meaning but misguided pleas we hear coming from pulpits today is the mantra, "Live your life for Christ!" To insist that the Christian life is about somehow "living for God" is to miss the point entirely! We have been crucified and raised with Christ and now the resurrected Jesus lives in and through us!

According to 2 Corinthians 5:17, to be "in Christ" (our root) is to be a "new creation; the old is gone, the new has come!" To say that we are a new creation is to say that our former sin nature is dead and buried. That nature has been exchanged for the new nature of Jesus Christ Himself.

A Point of Clarification

As a pastor who loves and often teaches from the 1984 edition of the New International Version (NIV) translation of the Bible, there is a major flaw that has caused confusion having to do with the translation of the word "flesh". The Greek word "flesh" in the NIV was inaccurately translated "sinful nature" throughout much of the New Testament. For many believers, this has created an unfortunate and consequential misunderstanding. Thankfully the most recent edition of the NIV translation has largely corrected this weakness.

Again, Scripture teaches that the moment we are "in Christ" by grace through faith alone, we become new creatures. The old is gone and the new has come. This "old" includes, but is not limited to, our "old nature" or "sin nature" that we inherited from Adam. Whenever a Christian talks about their supposed struggle with the "sin nature" they are grossly misunderstanding a very important reality: the sin nature no longer exists within a Christian. Of course, this reality leads to the natural question: *"If I no longer have a sinful nature, why do I still sin?"*

> Whenever a Christian talks about their supposed struggle with the "sin nature" they are grossly misunderstanding a very important reality: the sin nature no longer exists within a Christian.

The Reason We Sin

Suffice it to say that our struggle with sin as believers in Christ is *not* due to a lingering presence of the "sinful nature". Rather, it is due to the reality of something the New Testament identifies as "the flesh". Our "nature" speaks of our true, core identity. Our nature is essentially the composite of who we truly are, whereas the "flesh" is something different than who we really are in Christ, yet continues to cause us trouble.

It is apparent in the New Testament that the battle we face with our flesh is essentially a battle against the habits and coping mechanisms which bring us momentary pleasure or relief, apart from dependence upon Jesus. Because we live in a world where the sin nature of unbelievers is everywhere present, temptation is all around us to indulge in gratifying these fleshly impulses.[80] When we become new in Christ (the moment we are saved), this reality does not automatically erase the memory of habits we formed prior to trusting in Christ, many of which seem pleasurable in the moment.

For example, when someone has conditioned themselves to experience sexual pleasure in ways which are outside of God's intentions for their sexuality, becoming a Christian does not magically eliminate that memory of how temporarily pleasurable the hedonistic lifestyle once made them feel. While that lifestyle ultimately leads to emptiness and ruin, the newly recreated child of God may remain tempted by the momentary, yet fraudulent promises of satisfaction those behaviors elicit.

In harmony with Galatians 2:20, Paul gave us substantial teaching in Romans 6 for experiencing a victorious Christian life in practical terms. After affirming that the risen Christ is alive to God the Father, he says, "In the same way, count yourselves dead to sin but alive to God in Christ Jesus. Therefore (or "based upon this reality") do not let sin reign in your mortal body so that you obey its evil desires."[81]

Do you see how amazing this is? The key to overcoming the reign of sin in our mortal bodies is to count ourselves (or consider that we are) dead to sin by faith because God says it is so. It is not based upon our subjective feelings. It is not based upon any supposed evidence of a new squeaky-clean track record or even upon feeling like we're gradually improving in our behaviors. And it is not something we can experience by striving to "crucify" our sin nature when in fact our sin nature is *already crucified* with Christ and He has made us new creatures at the core!

Additionally, did you happen to notice what Paul says about sin? He says we will not obey "its" evil desires. Sin lives *in* you, but sin is *not* you! Your newly re-created *spirit* is one hundred percent righteous and desires the things of God. Your *flesh* is the container where sin lives – that powerful force that seeks to rob you of the peace and joy of a Spirit-led lifestyle. Your *soul* (mind, will and emotions) is caught in the middle and can be influenced to reflect either your spirit or your flesh at any given time.

1 Thessalonians 5:23 affirms that we are three-part beings, consisting of a human *spirit*, a *soul* and a *body* of flesh. We have already seen that as believers our spirit (or heart) is now totally new and righteous, desiring the very things God desires.

The Greek word for spirit is *pneuma* and is the inmost part of who we are as image-bearers of God. When Adam sinned, this image was defaced by sin and passed down to every human being throughout history. This is where our old "sinful nature" comes from. Sometimes Scripture also uses the word *heart* when speaking of our spirit, or innermost person.

When we receive Christ, that innermost person – scarred as it was by the sin we inherited from Adam – was the part of us that God crucified with Jesus. Romans 6:5 says that we were "united with Him in His death". We know that this union with Christ in death cannot be referring to our physical *bodies*, since we did not die physically with Him 2000 years ago.

We can also conclude that this is not speaking in reference to our *soul*. The soul is the Greek word *psuche* from which we get the words *psyche* and *psychology*. Our soul, then, is our psychology – the realm of our mind, will and emotions. In essence, the soul is our personality.

Did our psyches die with Christ? Not at all! Our personalities remain very much in tact after we receive Christ. Of course, there is a very real transformation of our attitudes and thinking that can begin to take place (Rom. 12:1-3), but that's a process and not an instantaneous act such as crucifixion.

This leaves us with only one other option – that it was our human spirit (our old, sinful nature that we inherited from Adam) that was crucified with Christ when we were saved. One of the central promises of the New Covenant is that when we receive the life of Christ through faith, God exchanges our old spirit or "heart" for a new one that is now "one spirit with Christ" (1 Cor. 6:17).

So why do we sin?

We sin because our soul is always in the balance of everyday choices between temptation (what our flesh wants) and true fulfillment (what our spirit desires). In any given moment on any given day, we make "soul-choices" either to gratify the flesh or to gratify the spirit. Sometimes we lose that battle by making wrong choices, which is why Paul speaks of the renewal of our minds as a continual process in this life (Rom. 12:1-3).

The "Gotcha" Game

Whenever I teach on the reality that "dying to self" is not part of the New Covenant life as so many of us have assumed, someone inevitably plays "gotcha'" by reminding me that the Apostle Paul once claimed that he dies "daily."

Yes, the Apostle makes this statement in 1 Corinthians 15:31. But this daily dying is presented in the context of the things he was suffering for Christ due to the persecutions and hardships he faced as an Apostle trying to survive in a culture that was viciously opposed to his message.

Paul was not stating this as though it were part of his daily regimen to somehow "become a better Christian"![82] In context, he was commenting to the Corinthians about his resolute commitment to the spread of the uncut gospel in a world that was highly hostile to the message of grace through faith in Christ. For this, Paul died "daily" (i.e. literally faced the threat of death routinely) for the message he preached.

So again, why do we sin if our sin nature is dead and gone the moment we trust in Christ's gospel? The Bible says it is because of our *flesh* – that element of human weakness that has not forgotten about the pleasures of sin. The flesh is all about that temporary ease of taking the path of least resistance even though we know in our spirit that it is not God's best for us.

And if what the Bible says about the flesh is true, then how do we stop sinning? By trying harder not to? Good luck with that! By building into our lives regimented disciplinary routines by which we "kill off" the sin nature? No! The sin nature has already been "killed off". Paul tells us that overcoming sin's reign in our lives involves not killing off – but *plugging in*. This is what Jesus referred to as "abiding" in Him.

Abiding in Christ

Technically, every believer in Christ is "plugged in" to Jesus. As a free gift, we have received an irreversible connection to and union with the life of Christ. At the same time, Jesus invites us to move beyond the objective knowledge of our connection to Himself as the Power Source – and into a subjective, conscious, experiential knowledge He refers to as *abiding*.

In John 15 there is a passage which – when properly understood – becomes one of the most reassuring and encouraging passages in the Bible. It affirms our irreversible security in Christ, and also invites us to enjoy that security to the fullest.

In the case of the original disciples, they were about to lose their very best friend. Understandably, they interpreted this as an extremely dark and dismal experience – and for a couple days, it would be! They were at a point where they needed some encouragement and reassurance in a very *big* way! And Jesus gave them what they needed in the following reassurance:

> I am the true vine, and my Father is the gardener. He cuts off
> every branch in me that bears no fruit, while every branch that

does bear fruit he prunes so that it will be even more fruitful. You are already clean because of the word I have spoken to you. Remain (abide) in me, and I will remain (abide) in you. No branch can bear fruit by itself; it must remain (abide) in the vine. Neither can you bear fruit unless you remain (abide) in me.

"I am the vine; you are the branches. If a man remains (abides) in me and I in him, he will bear much fruit; apart from me you can do nothing. If anyone does not remain (abide) in me, he is like a branch that is thrown away and withers; such branches are picked up, thrown into the fire and burned.[83]

These metaphors are very powerful, and needful of some explanation in bridging their power into our modern context. As with so many Bible verses, some teachers will tend to read a preconceived theological bias into what Jesus is saying here, painting Christ's words with a very different brush than He intended. In the concluding chapter, we will uncover the truth about Jesus' invitation to abide.

Chapter 12: At Ease! (Abiding in the Vine)

live and lead a church located only minutes away from one of the planet's premier wine-producing regions. California's Napa Valley is globally renown for its scenic landscapes and vineyards lush with some of the world's best grapes.

In ancient Israel, winemaking was not only a booming industry, but part of daily life. Jesus' illustration of the Vineyard as the basis for spiritual growth is meant to anchor us securely in the meaning of New Covenant discipleship. In order to get at what Jesus is saying in John 15:1-5, let's first get rid of some old myths that tend to linger in our theological circles.

There are those from a school of theology who promote the idea that a person can lose their salvation. This belief is called an *Arminian* idea – based upon the teachings of a man named Arminius. When Jesus makes mention of a branch being "cut off" or "thrown into the fire" – some from this school will tend to immediately read their theological bias into the passage, making the claim that Jesus is implying we can lose our salvation if we don't have fruit in our lives.

Then there are those from a more Calvinist school of thought – who do *not* believe that we can lose our salvation. These folks usually say that Jesus is referring to those who were never truly saved in the first place. In other words, they would say that these people merely *professed* faith in Christ, but never really *possessed* faith in Christ because their lack of fruit shows that they didn't persevere to the end. If you've read the previous chapters of this book, you might notice that this is a popular view among those who believe in Lordship Salvation.

There is a third option that is more consistent in avoiding this tendency to read a preconceived theological framework into what Jesus is actually saying. This third option would agree with the Arminian in the fact that Jesus is indeed talking about true believers in this passage, but would disagree that He is suggesting they can lose their salvation.

On the other hand, the third option also agrees with the Calvinist on the issue that a truly saved person can never lose their salvation, but would disagree with the idea that Jesus is speaking in this passage about those who were never really saved in the first place. So the context demonstrates that Jesus is speaking of people who *are* genuinely saved, and that He is *not* talking about a loss of salvation in this passage, but something else entirely.

Understanding Spiritual Growth: Four Realities from the Vineyard

The Connection Issue

The *first* thing Jesus affirms is that He is the only way to be *connected* to God. This may sound basic to those who are already believers, but it is truly the basis for everything. Jesus says in verse 1, *"I am the true vine, and my Father is the gardener..."*

We can see from this opening statement that *only* Jesus connects us to the life of the Father. As we noted earlier, it is through this life that we have the security of knowing that the *worst* things we could experience in this life are as close to hell as we will ever get!

I believe in a literal place called hell. As a pastor, it is never a fun message to preach about, especially in a politically-correct culture that often likes to candy-coat everything and make believe that God won't judge evil. Yet even though I agree with what Jesus taught about there being a place of everlasting punishment for those who reject the gospel, I also believe that the worst thing about hell is not the fire or the darkness or the weeping and gnashing of teeth or any of the other imagery the Bible uses.

There is something more horrifying that all of that. That horror is the *absence of fellowship with God* – the reality of never again having the chance to engage with or experience His manifest presence. So the key question to begin with when discussing the issue of spiritual growth is simply: *Am I connected to God through Jesus?* In other words *"Am I a Christian"?*.

If Jesus is who He claimed to be, then this is the most important question you will ever answer on this side of eternity. Jesus claims to be the *only* way to have a relationship with God. And in verse 1, He is echoing what He already stated back in chapter 14 when He said, *"I am the Way, the Truth and the Life – and no one comes to the Father except through Me."*[84]

The ancient Israelites understood their nation to be the only way to God. And they were partly correct. Originally, God had created Israel with that very mission – to be a kingdom of priests and a holy nation (Exodus 19:6). And what is the job of a priest? It is to serve as a *mediator* between God and humanity. So God's original mission for Israel was that they would be a light for the Gentiles in showing the world how to live in relationship with God.

For centuries, if you were a Gentile and you wanted to have a relationship with God, you needed to place your faith in the God of Abraham, Isaac and Jacob. So Jesus, by identifying Himself as the "true Vine," is telling His followers and also the entire world that they are no longer to look to the nation of Israel for their priesthood.

Israel is referred to throughout the Hebrew Scriptures as God's Vineyard (eg. Isaiah 5:7). In this scene from John 15, Jesus has the audacity to claim that *He* is the *true vine* from that Vineyard! That's quite a claim to make, as He was trying to get His Jewish followers to understand the *final* priestly sacrifice He was about to make by offering Himself on the cross!

The first step, then, on the road to abiding in Christ is simply to know that you're irreversibly connected to God through Jesus the

True Vine. This connection happens as a free gift, by grace through faith – apart from any human effort or works on the part of the believer (Ephesians 2:8-9).

The Commitment Issue

The *second* thing Jesus reveals is that we grow spiritually only because God is *committed* to our growth (John 15:2-3). I find it strange that so many preachers emphasize the idea of our "commitment" as the foundation of spiritual growth, when Jesus reveals that it is really God's commitment to *us* that matters most. Jesus goes on to say: *"He (God the Father) cuts off every branch in me that bears no fruit, while every branch that does bear fruit he prunes so that it will be even more fruitful."*

This phrase translated "cut off" is a misleading translation. It comes from the Greek word *airo*, which has three basic meanings:

1) to lift or pick up in a literal sense
2) to lift up in the figurative sense, such as "to lift one's soul"
3) to lift up in order to remove or carry away.

As I mentioned already, some folks have read the phrase "cut off" in the English translations, assuming that this must refer to either one of two things. Arminians believe this proves that you can lose your salvation. This is difficult to defend for multiple reasons, not the least of which is that just five chapters earlier in John 10, Jesus made the bold pronouncement that *none* of his "sheep" could be lost or plucked out of his hand.[85]

Then others from the more Calvinist persuasion have said that this must be referring to people who aren't genuinely saved in the first place. But this is also difficult to support when we consider that Jesus is giving this teaching to those He already knows for certain are genuinely saved. Judas has already left their presence, and Jesus is specifically referring to people who He says are "in Him" – a phrase that is *exclusively* used to describe genuine believers.

So what does this mean, then – this notion of being "cut off" in verse 2? Whenever we have a word with multiple possible meanings, we always look to the context in determining how the word is being used. Clearly, the context here demands a translation other than rendering it "cut off."

In viticulture, whenever a new branch emerges from a vine it has a tendency to hang down toward the ground. When a branch is hanging down toward the ground, it often doesn't get enough light. Additionally, it becomes covered with dust or coated with mud and mildew as the rains soak the vineyard. When this happens, the branch becomes weak and useless. In other words, it doesn't bear good fruit (if any fruit at all) when its hanging down along the ground!

Now what would an ancient vinedresser do when he or she encountered a branch like this? Cut it off? Wipe it out? You might think so, if you were to believe the mistranslation here in verse 2. But the vinedresser knows that the branch has much more potential than that.

In reality, the vinedresser would come through with a canister of water and first clean the dirt off the branch. Then he or she would carefully "lift up" the branch so that it would be exposed to proper light and nourishment. Charles Swindoll explains the process well when he writes…

> "…these two verses introduce the illustration in summary fashion, describing the general care of a vinedresser nurturing a vine. Vinedressers are rarely seen cutting off branches during the growing season. Instead, they carry a bundle of strings and pair of pruning shears as they work their way down a row. They carefully lift sagging branches and tie them to the trellis – a procedure called 'training'. They also strategically snip smaller shoots from branches in order to maximize their yield of fruit, which is called 'pruning'."[86]

Swindoll does a great job of explaining this process Jesus is describing and the way His original audience would have understood the metaphors. What this tells us is that Jesus is *not* suggesting that if we don't have enough so-called "fruit" in our lives to somehow "prove" or "legitimize" our Christianity, we're going to hell. In fact, He's saying the exact opposite!

Jesus is saying that God is *committed* to our spiritual growth process no matter what. The only "strings attached" are the ones the Vinedresser uses to hoist us up into the light! Paul told the Roman Christians in the midst of their suffering that God had *predestined* them to become conformed to the image of Christ! (Rom. 8:29-30)

In other words, God's plan for every believer from the foundation of eternity is to conform our lifestyles to manifest increasing expressions of Christ-likeness. Throughout the NT, we discover that we have a choice in the matter. We can either be dragged kicking and screaming or we can willingly let God do His work, but one way or another, God is going to mold us into the image of Christ. Of course we will not see the absolute finished product until the moment we pass from this life into eternity with Him, but we are on the path.

In response to this second reality, the key question to ask and answer would be: *Am I focused on my commitment to Jesus or His commitment to me?* Remember: security leads to maturity, not vice-versa! You will never begin to *feel* more secure in your faith by being overly focused on becoming a so-called "better Christian. That's a recipe for burn-out – and yet, this attitude is pandemic in the church today!

I mentioned earlier that spiritual insecurity has swept the church like wildfire. Under the guise of the "pursuit of holiness," believers in Jesus have become morbidly introspective about whether or not they're producing enough so-called "fruit". This preoccupation with performance causes many to live with a daily inability to ever feel like legitimate Christians!

Listen to what has been repeated many times already in this book: Your legitimacy is found in the unconditional promise of the Gospel – that if you *simply believe* on the Lord Jesus Christ you *will be saved*!

If your security is tied to your performance rather than to Christ's promises – you will *not* survive, much less thrive – in the Christian life! God has designed religious self-effort to be a major headache so that you will eventually give up on that approach and learn to abide in Jesus.

The discussion of the vine and the branches in John 15 is *not* a passage about salvation! This is a passage about discipleship – about spiritual growth – and about God's radical commitment to us in that process! How sad that so many Christians have misunderstood these verses to suggest that we might lose our salvation if we don't produce fruit, when Jesus is teaching the exact opposite!

The real message is simple: "Because you *are* saved – God is committed to your growth process. I (Jesus) just want to show you how to make it much more enjoyable and fulfilling. You can choose to go kicking and screaming, but I would offer you another way…"

Interestingly, nowhere in this passage does Jesus command His followers to produce fruit! The imperative in this passage, is to *abide* (or as the NIV translates it, "remain"). This word literally means "to dwell or live restfully or securely." It carries that same quality of restful trust that the Psalmist mentioned when he said, "Be still and know that I am God."[87] To abide is to live restfully, consciously and securely in Christ's loving presence! Some have called this "practicing the presence of God."

A branch doesn't produce fruit. A branch *bears* fruit as the result of the nourishing sap of the vine flowing into its outer extremities. Fruit-bearing happens from a position of rest, not stress. And that rest is something that all too commonly eludes those who believe in a version of the gospel other than the uncut version that Jesus and the Apostles taught.

The Conduit Issue

A *third* reality Jesus highlights in His tour of the vineyard is that Christian living is being a *conduit* of Christ's life (4-5). Jesus says *"No branch can bear fruit by itself… apart from me you can do nothing."* Simply abiding – consciously resting, living, dwelling in the nourishing sap of Jesus the Vine – is the most foundational reality of Christian living! Because of our fleshly tendency toward legalism, resting and enjoying our union with Christ is the toughest "work" many believers will ever learn to do.

Isn't that so true? For many, the most difficult thing about living the Christian life is simply learning to rest – to abide – in the all-sufficiency of Jesus Christ! Andrew Farley drives this home nicely in his book *Heaven is Now*, when he shares a devotional thought from the perspective of Jesus speaking to one of God's children. The conversation is fictional, yet drenched in the truth of Scripture as Jesus says

> Through my finished work, I have made you clean and close to me, and you are invited to live in a spiritual seventh day, relaxing in me. But to rest in me takes work. It's not the kind of work you're used to but a very different kind of work. I'm asking you to dig deeper into all that I've done for you so that you can more fully celebrate it, even when outwardly there seems only cause for pain.[88]

Abiding in Christ. Resting securely and "working" to discover the endless depths of His grace. This is the supreme goal of New Covenant discipleship. Grace is not the *entry-point* of the Christian faith, but *the entire point*! All else flows from this. We can turn this relationship into religion in quite a hurry if we're not careful, can't we?

Therefore, the key question in response to this reality would be: *Am I focused upon living the Christian life – or upon Jesus living the life through me?* The only way to live the Christian life successfully is to abide restfully in the Vine (Jesus) and allow Him to live the life through you by His Spirit.

This is God's *Plan A* for discipleship under the New Covenant. And guess what? There is no *Plan B*! Under the *Old* System, the very best a rabbi could offer to his students was to encourage them to imitate His way of life – to mimic his behavior – and to try to copy his lifestyle. But Rabbi Jesus offers us something infinitely better!

There is a serious problem with the well-intentioned "WWJD" mentality that so many of us operate by. The little bracelets went out of style years ago, but we still seem to carry around the mentality. We encounter a circumstance or a temptation and we try our best to discipline ourselves to say "What Would Jesus Do?" Then we white-knuckle our way through that circumstance trying to behave like we think Jesus would behave.

If we're lucky, we might not behave *quite* as sinfully as we would have had we not trained our brains to ask that question. But at the end of the day, we are operating in our own power! The focus is on *us* behaving properly rather than upon Christ *in* us, the hope of glory!

This is one major reason why so many well-meaning believers end up burnt-out, beat-up and broken-down with their version of Christianity – because it's not *real Christianity* in the first place. Real Christianity is not about trying to be good, but rather *Christ in me*, the hope of glory!

The Carnality Issue

When this breakdown happens, it can easily lead to the *fourth* reality Jesus highlights as He alerts His followers about what can happen when we don't abide in Him. Jesus says that it is possible to become *fleshly* instead of *fruitful* as believers. He goes on to say: *"If anyone does not remain in me, he is like a branch that is thrown away and withers; such branches are picked up, thrown into the fire and burned."*

We have already established that this passage is not a warning about losing salvation or going to hell. In this verse Jesus is affirming that it's possible for Christians to look hardly *any* different from the world – and about what a *tragedy* it is when that happens!

Jesus doesn't say that a person who fails to restfully abide in Him actually *is* a branch to be thrown away. He says that this person is *like* a branch that is thrown away. In other words, He is setting the stage for what James would later expand upon in James 2 when he says that faith without works is profitless. In other words, it doesn't bring much practical benefit to the real world.

You may be saved and on your way to Heaven, but God says that He has greater things planned for you in *this life* as well! He reveals that He has prepared some things to be accomplished through you and that He planned these things from the foundation of the world (Ephesians 2:10).

He says that you are an *ambassador* of His Kingdom on *this* earth…in *this* life…for such a time as *this!* There are a lot of what the Bible refers to as *carnal* (flesh-dominated) Christians roaming around planet earth who aren't restfully abiding in Christ, and therefore, they aren't bearing the kind of fruit God desires to produce through them.

Two Categories of Carnality:

Carnal Christians usually fall into one of two categories. The first category is what we could call *rebellious flesh*. This kind of carnality is the kind Paul addressed in 1 Corinthians 3:1-3:

> Brothers, I could not address you as spiritual but as worldly (literally "carnal")—mere infants in Christ. I gave you milk, not solid food, for you were not yet ready for it. Indeed, you are still not ready. You are still worldly ("carnal"). For since there is jealousy and quarreling among you, are you not worldly ("carnal")? Are you not acting like mere men?

In this passage Paul is rebuking the Corinthians for their *rebellious* carnality, echoing the words we just read from Jesus – that they were acting like *mere men* even though they were now believers. They weren't abiding in Christ, and therefore they weren't bearing good fruit.

As a pastor, I am asked to invest a lot of energy dealing with rebellious carnality in the church, mostly because its so obvious to identify when a person is walking in blatant rebellion against the ways of the Spirit. But there's another category of the flesh that is just as prevalent, and perhaps even more insidious. It's a kind of carnality we might call *religious flesh*.

Religious flesh was the kind of carnality that Jesus was always confronting in the Pharisees. Religious flesh was what the Apostle Paul was drawing attention to when he commented about how foolish he once was when he lived as a Pharisee, placing confidence in his outward, religious appearances. In Philippians 3:4-11, Paul makes this argument when he says

> If anyone else thinks he has reasons to put confidence in the flesh, I have more: circumcised on the eighth day, of the people of Israel, of the tribe of Benjamin, a Hebrew of Hebrews; in regard to the law, a Pharisee; as for zeal, persecuting the church; as for legalistic righteousness, faultless.

> But whatever was to my profit I now consider loss for the sake of Christ. What is more, I consider everything a loss compared to the surpassing greatness of knowing Christ Jesus my Lord, for whose sake I have lost all things. I consider them rubbish, that I may gain Christ and be found in him, not having a righteousness of my own that comes from the law, but that which is through faith in Christ—the righteousness that comes from God and is by faith.

So Paul talks to us about the reality of this *religious flesh* and about the fact that it is possible to deceive a lot of people – including yourself – into believing that your outward religious lifestyle is what counts! But Paul says, *no!* He considers all of that stuff flat-out *rubbish* (a word politely translated into English but in reality was the rough Greek equivalent to our "S-word").

In essence he says, "I was so foolish in those days when I was living to gain the applause of men rather than abiding in the applause of Jesus! That was all a load of crap!" And then he tells us what truly *is* important to him. Paul says

> I want to know Christ and the power of his resurrection and the fellowship of sharing in his sufferings, becoming like him in his death, and so, somehow, to attain to the resurrection from the dead.

In Christ, we have become like Him in His death – and we also share in the promise of His resurrection. When we abide (live restfully) in a conscious, daily awareness of His infinite love toward us, we bear the fruit of His Spirit, which is love (Galatians 5:22).

Freedom *To* or Freedom *From*?

Dr. Neil Anderson tells the story of a time he was invited to speak at a university on Christian morality in the context of family and marriage. One male student protested Dr. Anderson's lecture by sending all kinds of non-verbal cues of disgust and disinterest. At one point during the presentation a female student asked what Christians think about masturbation, to which the male student proudly exclaimed that he masturbated every day.

Awkwardly congratulating the outspoken young man, Dr. Anderson followed with the question, "Can you stop?" After class, a discussion ensued in which the student asked, "Why would I want to stop?" Anderson clarified that this was not his question. The question was "Can you stop masturbating?" and he went on to explain that what we often think is freedom is not really freedom at all, but slavery.[89]

When I served as a youth pastor, I encountered many similar discussions with students over the years. Often I would use alcoholism as an example. No alcoholic wakes up one random morning and decides, "Today is the day I will surrender my life to slavery!"

In the vast majority of cases, alcoholism begins with small, incremental expressions of "freedom" that eventually take over one's life – robbing them of peace, wreaking havoc on relationships and ultimately holding them captive to the very behaviors they once thought of as liberty.

Dr. Anderson rightly points out that our freedom in Christ brings liberty to our lives in three key areas: 1) Freedom from the Law, 2) Freedom from the past, and 3) Freedom from sin. Let's briefly consider each one.

Freedom from the Law

That we are free from the Law means a that couple of significant realities are in place. First, the New Testament teaches us that the Old System (the Law) is now "obsolete" for those who are in Christ (Hebrews 8:13). This means that like vinyl records, 8-tracks and VHS tapes, the Law is no longer in operation in our lives.

That the Law is now obsolete does not devalue its purity or usefulness. In fact, it does just the opposite! The Law is *so* pure and holy as a reflection of God's perfection that apart from Christ, humanity is crushed under the weight of it.

In Galatians 3, Paul describes the law as being like a "tutor" or "teacher". The actual Greek word is "pedagogue". In the ancient world, a pedagogue was like a nanny on steroids, hired by parents to strictly oversee the development of their children in almost every realm of life from education to social manners.

By using this term, Paul is informing us that the ultimate purpose of the Law was to crush us under the weight of its stringent demands, causing us to discover our need for Christ and driving us to His cross in faith.

A second reason we are free from the Law is because Jesus has already "fulfilled" the Law on our behalf. As often as this reality is reinforced throughout the New Testament, many Christians still don't get it. That Jesus "fulfilled" the Law on our behalf (Matt. 5:17) means that He lived the life we were incapable of living because of our

-   sin nature *before* we came to Christ and
-   our battles with the flesh *after* placing our faith in Christ.

As we emphasized earlier, Jesus not only died as our Substitute, but He also *lived* as our Substitute. There is no "pleasing" left to be done! We are already forever pleasing to our Heavenly Father because Christ's perfect record of obedience has been transferred to us even though on a practical level we continue to confront the habits of our flesh.

Understanding and accepting these realities are more than just subtle theological intricacies to be debated among theologians. They are crucial to understanding life in the Spirit. Since the battle begins "in the attitude of our minds" as we noted earlier, it is indispensable for us to immerse our minds in these truths on a regular basis.

Recently while attending an inter-denominational Christian baptism, one man asked the person being baptized, "Do you admit you are a filthy sinner saved by grace?" When our self-concept is centered upon the idea that we are "filthy sinners saved by grace" as so many Christians assume, we fail to bathe our minds in the reality of our new identity in Christ.

The phrase "sinner saved by grace" is not a New Testament designation for those who are "in Christ" by grace alone through faith alone. On the one occasion when Paul mentioned that he was the "chief of sinners", he was reflecting on his past career as a persecutor of Christians and not in reference to the new creation He had become through Christ.[90] This leads us to another precious reality...

Freedom from the Past

Not only are we completely forgiven of our sin and shame (as we have established throughout this book), but we are no longer identified in terms of bondage to sin's mastery over us. Galatians 4:7 says that when you are in Christ, you are "no longer a slave, but a child". This is the greatest possible news that a human being could receive! And yet, the passage goes on to say...

> Formerly, when you did not know God, you were slaves to those who by nature are not gods. But now that you know God – or rather are known by God – how is it that you are turning back to those weak and miserable principles? *Do you wish to be enslaved to them all over again*? (Galatians 4:8-9, emphasis mine).

Previously I argued that it is possible for genuine Christians to "fall from grace". Could it possibly be any clearer than in this passage? Paul is admonishing these Galatian believers – who were genuine children of God by faith in Christ – not to turn back to the "weak and miserable principles" of their former way of life. He even asks "Do you wish to be enslaved to them all over again?" Obviously Paul would never make such a statement if it were not a possibility for these saints to return to the slave-market of sin.

Falling from grace does not mean a "loss of salvation." Rather, because of our flesh it is possible for a truly saved person whose spirit is righteous and secure in Christ to become enslaved all over again! It means falling from the abundant life of grace that Jesus offers to each of His children as we "abide in Him" or "live by the Spirit". How tragic when this happens in the life of a believer!

In Christ, not only is your slate completely and eternally cleansed of all sin, but you are completely and eternally empowered to live in freedom from its reign over your life. Through faith in Christ, you are no longer a slave, a "filthy sinner saved by grace." You have a new heart, a new perspective and a new ability to walk in freedom from that which formerly held you in chains. This fact naturally leads into the third essential reality...

Freedom from Sin

That we are free from sin means that we no longer *have to* sin. Slavery is no longer our identity. Freedom is. And the only way we can possibly see real "fruit" from this reality is to rest in the "root" of our new identity. Remember, there is only one person in the entire universe who can live the Christian life successfully, and that person is Jesus. This means that as we begin to accept the crucified status of our sin nature, we make room for the life of Christ to take its place. Even though our flesh is strong, it is not strong enough to control us unless we invite it to do so.

> Remember, there is only one person in the entire universe who can live the Christian life successfully, and that person is Jesus.

Now if we died with Christ (which we have according to Paul's argument), we believe that we will also live with him.

For we know that since Christ was raised from the dead, he cannot die again; death no longer has mastery over him. (Romans 6:8-9)

Because we are in Christ and Christ is in us, what has no mastery over Christ has no mastery over us either. This message is true whether we fully grasp it or not. The Christian life then, is not accomplished by trying our best to please God. Rather it is found in surrendering by faith to the reality that we are *already as pleasing to God as we ever will be*, and that Jesus can and will live His life through us by the Spirit. For "sin shall not be (our) master, because (we) are not under the law, but under grace" (Rom. 6:14).

A Final Word

If you get nothing else from this book, my prayer is that you would understand this: Your Christian experience is both an event and a journey. The "event" is that based upon your faith in Christ's sacrifice, you are *irreversibly secure* in your salvation from the moment you believe, even if you stumble in and out of various degrees of doubt, sin, or other troubles. As James says, "We all stumble in many ways."[91]

You already have a place reserved for you in heaven and this is a free gift regardless of your performance as a disciple of Jesus. That this is true also means that upon trusting in Jesus for salvation, you have embarked upon a journey in which His Spirit will begin to work in your life.

The "journey" means that Jesus wants you to trust Him not just with your eternal destiny, but with your day by day, moment by moment relationship to the God who loves you so much that He would rather die than live without you – literally! He desires so much more for you than existing in the lowly mindset of a "sinner saved by grace". You are a blood-bought saint of the living God – a child of the King – a son or daughter who has been adopted and given the full rights and privileges of living as an heir of God.

The choice is yours. *First,* you can either receive or reject God's unconditional offer of salvation. Beyond this, there is another choice involving who will be in charge of your life. Do you want to be "enslaved all over again" to the things from which God has set you free? Or do you desire a quality of life that is higher and more rewarding than you could ever imagine?

I stand with Paul in praying that the eyes of your heart may be enlightened in order that you may know the hope to which he has called you! Paul explains this hope as being two-fold in Ephesians 1:15-23.

The first part is the "riches of His glorious inheritance in the saints" (that you will understand and long for that rich welcome you will receive when you stand face to face with Christ). The second is His "incomparably great power for us who believe" (that you will choose to abide in the grace and strength of His resurrection on a daily basis). You've been set free and therefore you are able to choose liberty!

May your mind and heart embrace a purer vision and understanding of God's grace than you ever thought possible! May you reject the front-loaded versions of the gospel that shackle you with preliminary requirements! May you ignore the back-loaded versions of the gospel that keep you bound with an obsessive focus on results! These human edits have effectually left the grace of God in shambles on the cutting room floor. May you never return to that yoke of bondage!

Instead, may you begin walking in the freedom of Christ while helping others discover the same! May you rest so fully in the grace and truth of Jesus Christ that the easy yoke of your Savior is the only yoke you bear!

Religion says: Earn your way, prove yourself, atone for your sins, feel guilty, be weary, hope that God will accept you, keep striving, do your best, behave properly, act happy, meet God halfway, He helps those who help themselves, try harder, produce good works, keep the rules, don't rock the boat, don't ask questions, promise to do better.

Jesus says: It is finished! Abide in me and you will bear fruit!

This is the true message of salvation and the Christian life!

This is the Gospel Uncut!

Bibliography

Chapter 1
[1] Courson, Jon, Through the Bible teaching on Galatians 1
[2] Acts 14:15
[3] Jude 3
[4] Manning, Brennan, *The Ragamuffin Gospel* (Sisters: Multnomah, 2005), 212
[5] McKnight, Scott, *The Blue Parakeet* (Grand Rapids: Zondervan, 2008), 29-37
[6] see Jude 3
[7] Romans 1:16-17
[8] This book was *The Gospel According to Jesus* by John F. MacArthur. While many other writings served to reinforce this view of the gospel during my earlier years of faith, this book was the catalyst for my initial formulation of those beliefs.

Chapter 2
[9] Isaiah 9:6-7
[10] 1 Timothy 3:16
[11] Matthew 5:20
[12] Matthew 9:12

Chapter 3
[13] Adherents to the system of theology espoused by Reformer John Calvin and his early followers.
[14] Acts 16:30-31
[15] MacArthur, John F., *The Gospel According to Jesus* (Grand Rapids: Zondervan, 1988), 140
[16] Galatians 5:16
[17] Romans 3:25; 1 John 2:2
[18] John 20:31

[19] see John 3:16; Acts 16:30-31; Romans 3:21-4:5; Galatians 3:6-9; Ephesians 2:8-9; Philippians 3:7-9, etc.

[20] Romans 7:7-25

[21] 1 Cor. 11:23-26

[22] John 1:11; Galatians 4:4

Chapter 4

[23] 1 Timothy 3:16-17

[24] 1 Corinthians 9:24; Philippians 3:14; 2 Timothy 4:7

[25] Keathley III, J. Hampton, *The Doctrine of Rewards,* © 1996 Biblical Studies Press (accessed online at www.bible.org). Much of the information contained in this section is influenced by or adapted from Keathley's article.

[26] MacArthur, John F., *The Gospel According to Jesus* (Grand Rapids: Zondervan, 1988), p. 31

[27] Bing, Charlie, accessed online:www.gracelife.org/resources/ gracenotes.asp?id=47

[28] Farley, Andrew, *The Naked Gospel* (Grand Rapids: Zondervan, 2009), 197-98

[29] Ibid., p. 198

[30] Hebrews 10:26-27

[31] Hebrews 1:3

[32] John 19:30

[33] Hebrews 8:6

[34] Galatians 1:10

Chapter 5

[35] Romans 5:20

[36] Piper, John , *"Why God is Not a Megalomaniac in Demanding to be Worshipped"* from the 60th Annual Meeting of the Evangelical Theological Society. Available through ACTS Conference Products, # EV08487 (www.actsconferenceproducts.com)

[37] Ibid.

Chapter 6

[38] Luke 15:1-2

[39] Lucas, Jeff, *The Prodigal-Friendly Church* (Grand Rapids: Zondervan, 2008), 59-61

[40] John 3:18

[41] Manning, Brennan, *The Ragamuffin Gospel* (Sisters: Multnomah, 1994), 22

[42] For a more thorough exploration of the story of the lost sons, I recommend *The Prodigal God* by Tim Keller

Chapter 7

[43] Romans 2:4

[44] Manning, Brennan, *A Glimpse of Jesus* (San Francisco, HarperCollins, 2003), 4-20

[45] Ibid., p. 5

[46] Ibid., p. 7

[47] Seamands, David A., *Healing for Damaged Emotions* (Colorado Springs: Cook, 2004), 78

[48] Manning, Brennan, *A Glimpse of Jesus* (San Francisco, HarperCollins, 2003), 9

[49] 2 Corinthians 7:10-11

[50] 1 John 2:1

[51] Wilhite, Jud, *Stripped: Uncensored Grace on the Streets of Las Vegas* (Sisters: Multnomah, 2006), 68-69

Chapter 8

[52] Romans 2:4

[53] John 15:5

[54] Galatians 5:22-23

[55] Dillow, Joseph C., *The Reign of the Servant-Kings* (Miami Springs: Schoettle, 1992), 21

[56] Ryrie, Charles C., *So Great Salvation*

[57] Farley, Andrew, *The Naked Gospel* (Grand Rapids: Zondervan, 2009), 149-150

[58] ibid. p. 150

[59] 2 Corinthians 7:10

[60] Matthew 11:28

Chapter 9

[61] 2 Corinthians 7:10-11

[62] Seamands, David, *Healing for Damaged Emotions* (Cook, etc.)

[63] Matthew 11:28-30

Chapter 10

[64] Colossians 2:13-15

[65] John 10:28-29

[66] 2 Corinthians 10:4

[67] Colossians 2:13-15

[68] Romans 8:37

[69] John 19:30

[70] Ephesians 2:14

[71] Luke 22:42

Chapter 11

[72] Revelation 20-22

[73] Packer, James I., *Concise Theology: A Guide to Historic Christian Beliefs* (Wheaton: Tyndale House, 1993), 160

[74] Grudem, Wayne, *Systematic Theology* (Grand Rapids: Inter-Varisty Press, 1994), 713

[75] Luke 23:32-43

[76] Nystrom, David P., *James: The NIV Application Commentary* (Grand Rapids: Zondervan)

[77] Chan, Francis, *Crazy Love* (Colorado Springs: David C. Cook, 2008), 83-84

[78] 1 Corinthians 1:26-31

[79] Zodhiates, Spiros, *Hebrew-Greek Key Study Bible* (AMG Publishing), 1488

[80] James 1:14

[81] Romans 6:11-12

[82] Read 1 Corinthians 15 for the entirety of Paul's argument here

83 John 15:1-6

Chapter 12
84 John 14:6
85 John 10:28-29
86 Swindoll, Charles R., *Insights on John* (Grand Rapids: Zondervan, 2010), 257
87 Psalm 46:10
88 Farley, Andrew, *Heaven is Now* (Grand Rapids: Baker, 2012), 16
89 Anderson, Neil T. and Quarles, Mike, *Overcoming Addictive Behavior* (Venura: Regal Books, 2003), 74-75
90 1 Timothy 1:12-16
91 James 3:2

Questions for Individual or Small Group Application

Chapter 1 – Contenders

1. What is legalism and why you think it is no less prevalent today than it was during the ministries of Jesus and the Apostles?
2. What is the difference between reading the Bible *with* tradition and reading the Bible *through* tradition? Why is it important to avoid the latter?
3. In what way(s) do you feel that the simple gospel of grace has been skewed – however slightly – in your spiritual journey thus far?
4. If you were asked to define "grace" succinctly, how would you explain it?
5. Why is contending for the gospel of grace so central to the uniqueness of the Christian life and message?
6. Read Galatians 1:6-9. Why was Paul so adamant about defending the gospel of grace from the perversions that were creeping into the church? How is this instructive for us in the church today?

Chapter 2 – Front-Loaders (Exposing the False-Gospel of Requirements)

1. From what you remember, what essentially does it mean to "front-load" the gospel with preliminary requirements?
2. Why is front-loading a direct attack on the gospel of grace?
3. In your own words, re-state the meaning of *repentance* based upon the information presented chapter 2.
4. Rather than a *Kingdom Manifesto* or *Constitution*

for Christian Living, what was Jesus' major point in preaching the Sermon on the Mount?

5. How does Matthew's Gospel account serve as a "bridge" between the end of the Old Covenant and the beginning of the New?

6. Why is it so important to understand the context of Jesus' words before trying to apply them to our lives?

Chapter 3 – Back-Loaders (Exposing the False-Gospel of Results)

1. From what you remember, what essentially does it mean to "back-load" the gospel with mandatory results?

2. It was stated in chapter 3 that our spiritual security is the basis of our spiritual maturity and not the other way around. Explain in your own words what was meant by this…

3. Biblical faith is "confidence" or "trust" that what God says is true on a personal level. Why is the Gospel account of John so strong in supporting the idea that simple faith (trust) in Christ is the only requirement for receiving salvation?

4. According to Hebrews 9:16-17, when did the New Covenant actually begin…at Jesus' birth or at His death? Why is this significant in understanding much of Jesus' teaching prior to the cross and resurrection?

Chapter 4 – God in the Hands of Angry Sinners?

1. In your own words, re-state some of what you learned about Romans 14:10 and the idea that Christians will stand before the "judgment seat".

2. In your opinion, does the idea of receiving a future

reward in any way negate or minimize the message of grace? Why or why not?

3. What is the major thrust of the book of James, and why is the James 2:14-26 passage so controversial?

4. How would you answer someone who makes the claim that "dead" faith means "phony" or "non-existent" faith?

5. Hebrews 10:26-27 is used by some to suggest a possible loss of salvation. Why is this idea so out of sync with the context of Hebrews 10 and the entire New Testemant?

Chapter 5 – Ruffling Feathers with the Grace of God

1. Why are some people so quick to caution believers not to esteem the grace of God "too highly". Is it even *possible* to do such a thing? Explain...

2. If by definition grace is radically imbalanced in our favor, why does there seem to be so much talk about "balancing" grace with calls to commitment, obedience, surrender, etc.?

3. What is the difference between the pre-cross message Jesus taught ("come and die") and the post-cross message the Apostles taught ("count yourself dead"). Why is this so critical to our understanding of grace-based discipleship rather than works-based?

4. Why is assurance of salvation *not* a matter of secondary importance, but critical to our growth as disciples of Jesus?

5. In your own life, how has the issue of assurance of salvation positively or negatively affected your spiritual journey?

Chapter 6 – The Gospel Jesus Revealed

1. In the story of the prodigal son, who or what is represented by the three main characters (the lost son, the father and the older brother)?
2. In this story, Jesus illustrates exactly what Paul said in Romans 2:4 – that God's kindness is what leads to a true change of mind and heart. How has the story of the prodigal son ministered to you personally in your spiritual life?
3. Besides what was presented in chapter 6, what other insights about the gospel of grace do you glean from Jesus' story?
4. It was noted that many folks resist coming to the Father not because they are unattracted to Jesus, but rather for fear of the "older brother". Have you ever been on either side of that equation?

Chapter 7 – Who Really Cares About Sin?

1. Why is believing that Christians are "forgiven no matter what" not the same thing as saying "God doesn't care about sin"?
2. Why is it that we can say with absolute confidence that God is not angry with His children, even when they sin?
3. If God's wrath against sin has been put to rest through Christ' sacrifice, then how *does* God feel when we sin? What *is* His disposition toward us when we are disobedient to Him?
4. In what way(s) have you struggled with the following...
    - » *Projectionism (projecting onto God your own ideas)*
    - » *Perfectionism (living with the "saint-or-sinner, all-or-nothing" mentality)*

» *Moralism/Legalism (believing God is happier with you on your "good days")*

» *Unhealthy Guilt (or "shame", believing that you are beyond His love)*

5. How was the building of the Golden Gate bridge an illustration of the practical power of grace in our lives?

6. How is "bearing fruit" different than "trying hard to please God"?

Chapter 8 – Myths and Legends

1. What was Jesus' point in telling His audience that if they didn't forgive others, God wouldn't forgive them? Why is this *not* an idea for New Covenant believers to live by?

2. Why is confession of sin *not* commanded as a way to maintain daily cleansing from God? Where does our cleansing actually come from? If confession does nothing to trigger ongoing forgiveness from God, then what is it's true purpose?

3. Why do we so freely use the word "convict" to describe the Holy Spirit's work in the lives of believers when the Bible doesn't use such terminology except referring to unbelievers?

4. If we began ascribing to the Holy Spirit the actual ministries the Bible *does* assign to Him (Counselor, Comforter, Helper, Advocate, etc.) what positive impact might this have upon the way we related to Him?

Chapter 9 – Resting or Wrestling?

1. In this chapter the author shares from his personal testimony about how Satan used sexual immorality to sink the claws of shame into his young soul. How

has the enemy waged a war of shame against you in your past?
2. Why is it so easy for those in positions of spiritual "leadership" to find themselves lonely, isolated and vulnerable to the attacks and lies of Satan?
3. Would you describe your own spiritual battles as having been fought primarily from a place of resting or wrestling? Explain...
4. How have the theological and spiritual influences in your life impacted your views on Satan, demons and spiritual warfare?

Chapter 10 – Relaxing on the Battle Field
1. Have you been exposed to the idea of "binding" or "rebuking" Satan as part of your Christian life? Why is such a practice so unwarranted based on the New Covenant?
2. What does it mean – in practical terms – to "put on the full armor of God" if we are already clothed with Christ?
3. How have the elements of armor listed by Paul been beneficial to you personally? Try to think of at least one specific example in which each piece has helped you...
  » *The Belt of Truth (rejecting lies from the enemy)*
  » *The Breastplate of Righteousness (standing in grace)*
  » *Feet Fitted with the Gospel of Peace (resting in His finished work)*
  » *The Shield of Faith (trusting God)*
  » *The Helmet of Salvation (longing for Christ's return)*
  » *The Sword of the Spirit (using the Word in your life)*

4. If the only real weapons remaining in Satan's arsenal are lies and deception, what does this tell us about the crucial practice of renewing our minds (Rom. 12:1-3)?

Chapter 11 – New Covenant Disciples (Grace to Obey)

1. Why is the concept of a "dual-natured Christian" so unbiblical and counter-productive to experiencing spiritual growth?

2. If our "sinful nature" was crucified with Christ and we truly are new and righteous at the core, why do we still struggle with temptation and sin?

3. What is the essential difference between merely a *changed life* and an *exchanged life*? Why is this understanding so critical?

4. What does it mean that we are not only saved by Christ's death, but also saved by His life (Rom. 5:10)?

5. Why does translating the word *flesh* as "sinful nature" often create such confusion surrounding the truth that we have a single, righteous and redeemed nature at the core of our being?

Chapter 12 – At Ease! (Abiding in the Vine)

1. What does it mean to "abide in Christ"? Why is abiding the key to growth as a New Covenant disciple?

2. What is the difference between living as a disciple under the Old Covenant and living as a disciple under the New Covenant, and how does Jesus' teaching on the Vine and the Branches illustrate this?

3. Many modern Christian teachers emphasize our commitment to Christ when Jesus seemed to place the emphasis on God's commitment to us. How might focusing on the latter actually have a more positive affect on the former?

4. Of the two categories of flesh (rebellious and religious), where do most of your struggles come from – or are they about equal? Why do you think this is the case?

5. Summarizing in your own words, what does it mean to experience freedom from...
   » *The Law?*
   » *The past?*
   » *Sin?*

6. How has the content of this book challenged your thinking about what it means to live the Christian life?

About the Author

Jeremy White lives in Northern California with his wife April and their three boys. After serving 15 years in youth ministry, he transitioned to the role of Lead Pastor at Valley Church in Vacaville in 2009. Forever a youth pastor at heart, Jeremy continues to write youth ministry articles and curriculum aimed at setting students free with the uncut gospel. His grace-proclaiming weekly messages can be heard at www.valleychurch.com. You can also follow his blog at www.thegospeluncut.blogspot.com or find him on Facebook. *The Gospel Uncut* is Jeremy's first book. If you like the book, please drop him a note on Facebook or at jwhite@valleychurch.com. As a full-time pastor, he cannot guarantee a personal response to all email – although he will try his best!